Facing the Missile Challenge

U.S. Strategy and the Future of the INF Treaty

David W. Kearn, Jr.

Supported by the Stanton Foundation

The research described in this report was supported by the Stanton Foundation.

Library of Congress Cataloging-in-Publication Data is available for this publication.
ISBN: 978-0-8330-7682-3

The RAND Corporation is a nonprofit institution that helps improve policy and decisionmaking through research and analysis. RAND's publications do not necessarily reflect the opinions of its research clients and sponsors.

RAND® is a registered trademark.

Published 2012 by the RAND Corporation
1776 Main Street, P.O. Box 2138, Santa Monica, CA 90407-2138
1200 South Hayes Street, Arlington, VA 22202-5050
4570 Fifth Avenue, Suite 600, Pittsburgh, PA 15213-2665
RAND URL: http://www.rand.org/
To order RAND documents or to obtain additional information, contact
Distribution Services: Telephone: (310) 451-7002;
Fax: (310) 451-6915; Email: order@rand.org

Preface

The Intermediate Nuclear Forces Treaty (INF), signed in 1987, eliminated nuclear and conventional ground-launched ballistic and cruise missiles with ranges between 500 and 5,500 kilometers from the United States and Soviet arsenals. The treaty was a diplomatic watershed, signaling the beginning of the end of the Cold War. It has since served as a basis for security and stability of Europe. However, the security environment confronting the United States has dramatically changed in the past 20 years. Russia, while continuing to abide by the treaty, has revised its military doctrine to include the possibility of using nuclear weapons first to promote its interests in its "near-abroad" —the independent republics and nearby Eastern European countries —and raised the possibility of abrogating the Treaty. China has developed a robust short- and intermediate-range missile force, which contributes to a growing anti-access/area denial capability. Together with the deployment of advanced air, sea, and cyber-based assets, the Chinese missile force confronts the United States with a challenge to its ability project power in East Asia. Missile programs (ballistic and cruise) have expanded in other countries around the world, including proliferators such as North Korea and Iran, and regional rivals Pakistan and India.

The objective of this study is to assess whether the INF Treaty continues to serve American national interests, or whether adherence unduly constrains the ability of the United States to effectively respond to emerging security threats arising from the proliferation of intermediate-range missile systems. To answer this question, the study analyzes the challenges confronting the United States from Iran, North

Korea, India, Pakistan, and China, and considers the potential role that a future U.S. land-based intermediate-range conventional ballistic missile system could play in effectively addressing these challenges. Existing and potential programmatic alternatives also will be considered to present a comprehensive assessment of the potential utility and ultimate military contribution of such a program.

In order to develop and deploy a new generation of land-based intermediate-range ballistic missiles, the United States would have to withdraw from the INF Treaty. Such a diplomatic action would have significant political and military implications. The study attempts to explore and illuminate some potential responses of critical international actors, such as Russia, China, and America's NATO and East Asian allies, to fully understand the expected costs that may be incurred by the United States over time. Finally, the study concludes with a consideration of potential ways forward for the United States to provide policymakers with guidance on how to proceed in both diplomatic and political-military terms to best address the threat from missile proliferation.

This research should be of interest to military, government, and civilian planners, analysts, and scholars working on issues related to missile proliferation, arms control, and key regional security threats confronting the United States, including the challenge of Chinese military modernization and the Taiwan Straits.

Stanton Nuclear Security Fellows Program

The research reported here was prepared as part of the Stanton Nuclear Security Fellows program at the RAND Corporation. Research was conducted during a one-year fellowship at RAND under the guidance and supervision of a RAND mentor. This fellowship is financed by the Stanton Foundation. The author of this report thanks the input of colleagues and reviewers for improvements to the report, but any remaining errors or omissions are the sole responsibility of the author.

Comments are welcome and may be addressed to kearnd@ stjohns.edu.

Contents

Figures

Tables

Summary

Background

This study examines the question of whether the Intermediate Nuclear Forces (INF) Treaty continues to serve the security interests of the United States more than two decades after the Treaty's signing. Weapon systems that the Treaty explicitly prohibits, land-based intermediate-range (500 to 5,500 km) ballistic and cruise missiles—whether conventionally or nuclear-armed—have emerged as central assets in the arsenals of a number of critical regional powers. These missiles present significant threats to U.S. forces abroad and allies, begging the question: Does the United States require similar capabilities, currently proscribed under the INF Treaty, to effectively respond to these challenges? If the answer is "yes," then the constraints of the INF Treaty may, in fact, undermine U.S. national security interests. Conversely, given the extensive conventional military capabilities of the United States, there may be programs that can better address the threats of regional INF missiles forces in more cost-effective and operationally flexible ways.

The study will assess the nature of the regional security threats confronting the United States, utilizing an analytical framework derived from previous RAND research on deterrence in regional contexts. In doing so, the study will consider the effectiveness of existing programs that are likely to be available to decisionmakers to address these threats, as well as the potential contribution of a new generation of conventional U.S. land-based intermediate-range missiles moving forward. The study also examines the larger political and security ramifications of a U.S. withdrawal from the Treaty based on a consideration of interests of key regional allies and partners, and considers the potential diplomatic way forward for the United States.

Findings of the Study

Defining the Challenge of Missile Proliferation

Over the past decade, the character of missile proliferation has been primarily *vertical*, reflecting the qualitative advancement of existing missile programs rather than the spread of new programs associated with *horizontal* proliferation. Multilateral initiatives such as the Missile Technology Control Regime (MTCR) and the Proliferation Security Initiative (PSI) have increased barriers to the acquisition of ballistic missiles and associated technologies and the technical expertise and knowledge required to build extensive programs. Nonetheless, intermediate-range ballistic missiles have become key assets for regional powers such as Iran, North Korea, India, Pakistan, and China.

Addressing the Challenge of Intermediate-Range Missiles in Key Regional Contexts

While states like Iran and North Korea both present formidable threats to U.S. interests and those of its allies, it is not clear that the United States requires the "in-kind" capability to effectively deter those states or sufficiently defend its regional interests should deterrence fail. U.S. conventional military superiority, supported by a credible nuclear deterrent, as well as increasing missile defense capabilities and strong working relationships with formidable regional allies, provide capabilities necessary to effectively address these two difficult challenges. Similarly, while stocks of nuclear-armed intermediate-range missiles have increased in the arsenals of India and Pakistan, U.S. missiles seem an inappropriate remedy.

Addressing the Challenge of China's Missile Modernization

Ultimately, the only threat to U.S. security interests that could conceivably warrant serious consideration for withdrawing from the INF Treaty is the significant expansion, in both quantitative and qualitative terms, of the intermediate-range conventional missile forces of the People's Republic of China (PRC). These missile forces contribute to a growing Anti-Access/Area Denial (AA/AD) capability that could significantly degrade the capacity of the United States to effectively execute a campaign to defend Taiwan in the event of a conflict, and may undermine the ability of the United States to deter China from initiating hostilities in the event of a crisis.

Assessing the Case for U.S. Land-Based Intermediate-Range Conventional Ballistic Missiles

While an "in-kind" response to China's missile-centric military modernization program may seem particularly useful in holding at risk high-value targets (deployed mobile missiles, air bases, and command and control), the program likely would be relatively costly. Moreover, other issues—including limited basing options and likely Chinese responses to such a deployment—significantly decrease its perceived benefits. Other programmatic choices can be made to maintain or enhance U.S. conventional capabilities in the short-, medium-, and longer-terms that may be preferable in terms of cost-effectiveness and operational flexibility. In short, a new land-based intermediate-range conventional missile is unlikely to provide a silver bullet in responding to the threat of China's missile expansion.

The Political-Military Costs of Withdrawing from the INF Treaty

This study concludes that the political and security costs of a U.S. withdrawal from the INF Treaty likely would be significant and far-reaching. It is difficult to envision a scenario in which the military benefits provided by land-based conventional intermediate-range missiles would outweigh the political/military costs of withdrawal.

- **Russia.** While Russia may welcome the unfettered ability to reconstitute its intermediate-range forces, the reversal of current cooperative arms control trends is likely to raise Russian suspicions of U.S. motives, and the challenge of competing with the United States in another realm is not necessarily attractive. In short, it should not be assumed that the new freedom from Treaty restrictions would be interpreted as a benign signal, particularly in the longer term. Moreover, expansion of Russian capabilities to implement a military doctrine that relies on the first use of nuclear weapons would seem to create more problems than it solves.

- **Europe/NATO.** A clear and overwhelmingly negative response should be expected from Europe. Withdrawal from the INF Treaty would seem to reverse any momentum toward reducing non-strategic nuclear weapons in Europe, something many NATO members support. Acute concerns about a new Russian threat may exacerbate divisions between Western and Central European (or newer and older) members. At a more basic level, a decision to withdraw from an agreement that has underpinned the security and stability of Europe since the end of the Cold War would be seen as a further example of Washington's drift away from the alliance and its commitment to Europe's security interests.

- **East Asia.** Assuming current trends, and absent any clear Chinese provocations or a dramatic shift toward aggressive behavior, it may be difficult for the United States to justify the withdrawal from the INF Treaty in order to deploy conventional INF missiles in the region. Given the high levels of economic interdependence and the central role that China has assumed in regional trade flows, even U.S. allies such as Japan and South Korea are unlikely to be supportive of a diplomatic move that could be seen as provocative and undermining regional stability. Moreover, placing these states in the difficult position of making a clear choice in a potential conflict may precipitate significant domestic political turmoil, which likely would limit U.S. basing options to U.S. territories, such as Guam.

- **Global non-proliferation.** Finally, in terms of the broader global nonproliferation architecture, U.S. withdrawal from the INF Treaty is likely to undermine the MTCR and could spur further proliferation. While the MTCR has not been perfect, horizontal proliferation has been constrained since the late 1980s. A perceived reversal of U.S. leadership could damage the credibility of the regime. Moreover, two major potential suppliers, China and Russia, as well as a potential second class of suppliers made up of states outside the current regime, could have strategic and economic incentives to sell proscribed missile systems or withhold cooperation on nonproliferation initiatives.

The Way Forward

Because of the likely political and security costs, and the limited military benefits of land-based intermediate-range missiles in addressing the challenge of China's military modernization, it is difficult to envision the unilateral withdrawal from the INF Treaty as serving U.S. national interests. Instead, the United States should focus on working with Russia, and leverage Russian concerns about INF missile forces to expand the Treaty to countries such as China, India, Pakistan, and others. In the short term, the likely success of such a strategy is low, but it may provide a more suitable basis for a dialogue with Beijing than a focus on strategic weapons. In the interim, the United States should work with Russia to maintain the INF Treaty and, if necessary, address the potential problem of China's missile programs with alterative military programs that are better suited to the geography and political realities of East Asia and that may prove less costly.

Acknowledgments

First and foremost, the author wishes to thank Lynn Davis for all of her help on this project. She provided important insights and advice and carefully read and commented on previous versions of the draft, and her guidance and support were invaluable. Lowell Schwartz and Adam Stulberg provided detailed reviews of a previous draft that has greatly improved the final product. Thanks to Andy Hoehn and Paula Thornhill for their support and encouragement throughout the course of the fellowship. Robert Reardon and Markus Schiller were excellent colleagues and critical in helping along the development of the study. Many RAND colleagues provided support for the project, including Steve Larabee, James Quinlivan, Alan Vick, Lauren Caston, Jeff Engstrom, Jeff Martini, Ali Nader, Stacie Pettyjohn, and Ely Ratner. Special thanks to Sarah Harting for all of her help throughout the fellowship and the process of refining the study. Outside of RAND, Evan Montgomery was a reliable sounding board and insightful critic. Finally, I greatly appreciate the generous support of the Stanton Foundation and Liz and Graham Allison.

Abbreviations

AA/AD	Anti-Access/Area Denial
ABM	Anti-Ballistic Missile Treaty
ALCM	Air-Launched Cruise Missile
ASBM	Anti-Ship Ballistic Missile
ASCM	Anti-Ship Cruise Missile
ASW	Anti-Submarine Warfare
BMD	Ballistic Missile Defense
C4ISR	Command, Control, Communications, Computers, Intelligence, Surveillance, and Reconnaisance
CD	Conference on Disarmament
CFE	Treaty on Conventional Armed Forces in Europe
DPRK	Democratic People's Republic of Korea
GBI	Ground-Based Interceptor
GCC	Gulf Cooperation Council
GLCM	Ground-Launched Cruise Missile
ICBM	Intercontinental Ballistic Missile
INF	Intermediate-Range Nuclear Forces

ICOC	International Code of Conduct Against Ballistic Missile Proliferation
IRBM	Intermediate-Range Ballistic Missile
JASSM	Joint Air-to-Surface Standoff Missile
JASSM-ER	Joint Air-to-Surface Standoff Missile-Extended Range
LACM	Land Attack Cruise Missile
LRTNF	Long-Range Theater Nuclear Forces
MTCR	Missile Technology Control Regime
NATO	North Atlantic Treaty Organization
NFU	No First Use
NPR	Nuclear Posture Review
NSNW	Non-Strategic Nuclear Weapons
PAA	Phased Adaptive Approach (to Missile Defense)
PGM	Precision-Guided Munitions
PGS	Prompt Global Strike
PLA	People's Liberation Army
PRC	People's Republic of China
PSI	Proliferation Security Initiative
ROC	Republic of China
ROK	Republic of Korea
SLBM	Submarine-Launched Ballistic Missile
SLCM	Submarine-Launched Cruise Missile
SLV	Satellite Launch Vehicle
SSBN	Ballistic Missile Submarine

SSGN	Guided (Cruise) Missile Submarine
START	Strategic Arms Reduction Treaty
TBMD	Theater Ballistic Missile Defense
TEL	Transporter Erector Launcher
TLAM	Tomahawk Land Attack Missile
TNF	Theater Nuclear Forces
UAE	United Arab Emirates
UN	United Nations
UNSC	United Nations Security Council
WMD	Weapons of Mass Destruction

CHAPTER ONE
Introduction

The Intermediate Nuclear Forces Treaty (INF) eliminated nuclear and conventional ground-launched ballistic and cruise missiles with ranges between 500 and 5,500 km from the arsenals of the United States and the Soviet Union.[1] At the time of its signing in 1987, the Treaty was a diplomatic watershed, signaling the beginning of the end of the Cold War. It has since served as a basis for the security and stability of Europe, which is a vital security interest of the United States.

However, in the past 20 years, the security environment confronting the United States has changed. Missile proliferation, specifically missiles with ranges proscribed by the INF Treaty, has presented new challenges to U.S. interests in several key regional contexts. Countries with troubling proliferation records such as North Korea and Iran have engaged in extensive missile development programs, and missiles have become an increasingly important component of the India-Pakistan strategic rivalry. Perhaps most importantly, the People's Republic of China (PRC) has acquired a robust theater missile force, which contributes to a growing anti-access/area denial capability that could undermine the U.S. capacity to project power in the region and effectively respond to a crisis over Taiwan.[2] More generally, the proliferation of missile programs (ballistic and cruise) threatens to increase the number

---

[1] Missiles are generally categorized as follows: short-range (less than 1,000 km), medium-range (1,000-3,000 km), intermediate-range (3,000-5,500 km), and intercontinental (over 5,500 km).

[2] For the purposes of discussion, intermediate-range missiles will denote those covered in the INF Treaty (ranges 500-5,500 km). "INF missiles" will be used interchangeably.

of states with INF capabilities and further complicate regional security relationships. The perceived utility, cost-effectiveness, and technological feasibility of these systems have called into question the relevance and utility of the INF treaty, with some experts arguing that perhaps the Treaty no longer serves U.S. interests.[3] In their view, to adequately address these threats, the United States requires its own land-based intermediate-range missiles to maintain or enhance U.S. conventional military superiority in critical regions and deter behavior by regional powers armed with INF missiles that threaten American security interests. While some experts may be skeptical of arms control cooperation in general, the emerging threats to U.S. interests in key regional contexts, particularly the challenge of China's expansive short- and intermediate-range missile capabilities, make this study timely and salient.[4]

Focus of the Study

This study examines whether the INF Treaty continues to serve the security interests of the United States more than two decades after its signing. Land-based intermediate-range missile systems have emerged as central assets in the arsenals of a number of critical regional powers—threatening U.S. forward-based forces—and regional allies. This begs the question: Does the United States require similar capabilities, currently proscribed under the INF Treaty, to effectively respond to these challenges? If the answer is "yes," then the constraints of the INF Treaty may, in fact, undermine U.S. national security interests

---

[3] John R. Bolton and Paula A. DeSutter, "A Cold War Missile Treaty That's Doing Us Harm: The U.S.-Soviet INF Pact 'Doesn't Address the Iranian Threat,'" *Wall Street Journal*, August 15, 2011, p. 11; Kevin Ryan, "Expand or Scrap the Missile Ban: A Cold War Treaty Has Opened a Gap in U.S. and Russian Security," *Los Angeles Times*, October 16, 2007.

[4] The potential utility of a U.S. IRBM, proscribed under the INF Treaty, has been increasingly considered as a hypothetical response to China's missile programs. See for example, Andrew S. Erickson and David D. Yang, "On the Verge of a Game-Changer," *Proceedings Magazine*, Vol. 135, No. 5, 2009; Andrew Krepinevich, *Why Airsea Battle?* Washington: Center for Strategic and Budgetary Assessments, 2010; David A. Shlapak et al., *A Question of Balance: Political Context and Military Aspects of the China-Taiwan Dispute,* Santa Monica: RAND Corporation, MG-888-SRF, 2009.

and would logically warrant consideration of withdrawing from the Treaty. Of course, any comprehensive analysis of the contribution of the INF Treaty also must include an assessment of the potential political and security costs of withdrawal from the Treaty. Before turning to these questions, it is necessary to assess the current and potential threats to U.S. security interests created by the proliferation of intermediate-range missile systems.

Despite concerns about widespread general proliferation in the late 1990s and the possible emergence of many new missile-capable powers, the trends have been played out somewhat differently. Over the past decade, we have witnessed significant *vertical* proliferation—states with extant programs improving their capabilities in quantitative and qualitative terms—rather than the *horizontal* proliferation, or the spread of weapons to new actors. This seems to support the idea that multilateral initiatives like the Missile Technology Control Regime (MTCR), the International Code of Conduct against Ballistic Missile Proliferation (ICOC) and Proliferation Security Initiative (PSI) have had a positive effect of increasing barriers of entry for new proliferators. However, where states already possessed significant capabilities as of the mid-to-late 1990s, we have seen expansions of existing programs, particularly in the area of land-based intermediate-range ballistic missiles—those proscribed under the INF Treaty and thus banned from U.S. and Russian arsenals. These systems have become increasingly important components in the strategic programs of both India and Pakistan and are also critical to regional powers such as Iran and North Korea, allowing them to deter military interventions by conventionally superior powers like the United States and influence regional politics.

Perhaps the most acute threat to U.S. security interests arising from the proliferation of missile technology is the dramatic expansion of China's conventional missile forces. The buildup of ballistic and cruise missiles confronts the United States with a significant challenge:

- In the short term, China's missile capabilities may be utilized to effectively disarm Taiwan by knocking out its air force and seizing air superiority over the Taiwan Straits.

- China's growing stocks of intermediate-range ballistic and cruise missiles play a central role in what has been termed an anti-access/area denial strategy that would target U.S. forward bases and naval assets in the region to degrade the ability of the United States to effectively defend Taiwan.
- Over time, China could place nuclear warheads on some component of its intermediate-range ballistic and cruise missile forces, which are generally reported to be dual-use in design, thus significantly increasing the threat to U.S. allies in the region in a very short period. While this is regarded as a lower-probability threat, it deserves consideration simply because of the sheer number of delivery vehicles at China's disposal and the potentially significant political implications of a rapid increase in theater nuclear weapons that could be deployed in the region.

Because China's modernization efforts threaten key sources of U.S. military strength in the region—forward bases, tactical airpower, and naval assets—the ability of the United States to project power in the Western Pacific and to deter Chinese military operations has seemingly been compromised. Moreover, the quantitative expansions of China's missiles essentially have made U.S. ballistic missile defense cost-ineffective and unlikely to provide any more than a marginal contribution to defending forward-based assets in the event of a coordinated, large-scale attack.

In this context, experts have offered the United States' deployment of land-based conventional intermediate-range missiles as a potentially effective counter to China's missile buildup. Such a deployment would enhance U.S. conventional capabilities in the region, and thus rectify the perceived imbalance in forces across the Taiwan Straits. Advocates view the attributes of a conventional ballistic missile, specifically its ability to penetrate defenses and survive a first-strike, as a particularly appropriate countermeasure. These missiles, deployed in sufficient quantities, would hold high-value Chinese targets at risk, including their missile forces, air bases, and command and control. This would enhance the ability of the United States to defend Taiwan in the event of a crisis and thus deter a Chinese attack in the first place by increasing the expected costs and risks for Chinese planners. According to these experts, such forces deployed in the theater also would be less escalatory than potential U.S. military responses to a crisis that rely on "central" strategic systems, such as conventional submarine-launched ballistic missiles (SLBM) or perhaps a conventional intercontinental ballistic missile (ICBM) or other conventional prompt global strike (PGS) system.

However, despite these potential benefits, the United States may have other program options that can more effectively improve U.S. conventional military capabilities in terms of cost, operational flexibility, and crisis stability. Given the potential costs of a new intermediate-range ballistic missile program and the likely time before such a system could be procured, other assets that could enhance U.S. conventional military capabilities—and thus deter a Chinese attack or increase the risk or decrease the perceived benefits of an attack through denial or defense—should be considered. Ultimately, some mix of capabilities to deter and deny China in the short, medium, and long term may prove more effective than land-based intermediate-range missiles. This study will assess the potential contributions and costs of a new missile system, as well as existing and potential future alternative programs that could be employed to address China's missile threat.

Beyond assessing the potential military benefits of such a deployment, this study also will examine the likely political and military costs of decision by the United States to withdraw from the INF Treaty. Given that the last U.S. and Soviet INF missiles were destroyed 20 years ago, the salience of the Treaty has somewhat faded into the history of the end of the Cold War. Nonetheless, it is clear that the INF Treaty has played a critical role in providing stability and security to Europe during a time of major geopolitical transition and remains vital. Moreover, the destruction of these weapons precluded any shift in the superpower competition to places such as East Asia, contributing to a peaceful and stable regional security environment. Finally, the destruction of the intermediate-range systems and their development and production infrastructure contributed to the cause of nonproliferation by removing a potential source of additional missiles, components, and associated technologies from the international market. In short, while the benefits of the Treaty seem somewhat abstract today, a discussion of the potential costs of withdrawal actually presents the benefits it has provided in stark relief.

Finally, the study considers potential ways forward to guide policymakers' deliberations in both the short term and longer term. Given the assessment of the potential military benefits of the development and deployment of a new generation of land-based intermediate-range conventional ballistic missiles in contrast to other existing or potential programmatic options, and considering the potential political and security costs of withdrawal from the INF Treaty, the study presents policy options for decision-makers to consider.

Structure of Analysis

In order to comprehensively analyze the complex issues associated with this important topic and develop useful policy guidance, the study is structured as follows:

Step 1. Evaluate trends of missile proliferation

With more than a decade of efforts to stem the proliferation of missiles and associated technologies, the report has an opportunity to consider and evaluate trends that have emerged during that period. Focusing on the dynamics of horizontal versus vertical proliferation; the ability of states to obtain technical assistance; and the effectiveness of multilateral regimes like the MTRC, the Geneva International Code of Conduct for the Proliferation of Ballistic Missiles, and the U.S.-sponsored Proliferation Security Initiative, the study is able to more accurately construct a set of concrete and specific regional missile threats to the United States.

Step 2. Assess key INF missile threats to U.S. security interest

The proliferation of intermediate-range ballistic and cruise missiles has contributed to the threats posed by several key regional powers that threaten U.S. security interests and those of key allies. With North Korea's small nuclear weapons program, intermediate-range missiles provide its regime with the ability to hold U.S.-deployed forces and allies in East Asia at risk, increasing the potential costs of a conflict with what has been a historically risk-acceptant regime. Similarly, intermediate-range missiles provide the Iranian regime with a conventional power projection capability that could be used to retaliate against U.S. forces in the Middle East and/or intimidate or coerce regional allies in the event of a crisis or conflict. In the event Iran achieves a nuclear capability, its stock of intermediate-range missiles may provide a delivery capacity that will dramatically increase the threat within and beyond the region. On the subcontinent, IRBMs have assumed an increasingly important role in the strategic rivalry between India and Pakistan. Without being a direct threat to U.S. interests, these programs may increase the risk of escalation, reaching perhaps to the level of a nuclear exchange in the event of a crisis. Finally, a critical component of China's military modernization program is its significant expansion of short- and intermediate-range missile programs. Taken together with its larger modernization efforts, China's capacity to coerce or intimidate Taiwan has grown over the past decade. Perhaps more troubling is the expansion of intermediate-range missile systems (both ballistic and cruise) that allow China to hold U.S. forward-deployed forces in the region at risk. The implication is that, over time, the ability of the United States to effectively respond to a conflict over Taiwan is decreasing, which may undermine its ability to deter an attack in the first place.

To assess the nature of these threats in a comprehensive way, the study will utilize a model of regional deterrence based on previous RAND studies, derived from the larger deterrence literature. Focusing on the critical components of commitment and capability, the study examines the deterrent postures of the United States in the contexts of North Korea, Iran, and China. Having considered the capabilities available (and likely to be available) to the United States in addressing these challenges of deterring regional threats, the study considers the potential contribution of U.S. intermediate-range missiles to deterrent missions in light of other possible programmatic alternatives.

Step 3. Analyze likely costs of INF Treaty withdrawal or revision

Building upon the respective assessments of the regional threats arising from intermediate-range ballistic and cruise missiles, the study attempts to consider and analyze the potential costs associated with a U.S. withdrawal from the INF Treaty or a significant revision of the Treaty with Russian cooperation. Given the contribution of the INF Treaty to the U.S.-Russia relationship, security in Europe, and other key regional considerations, the task of analyzing the potential costs of withdrawal from the Treaty will focus on several specific questions. Specifically, a significant transformation or ending of the Treaty will be assessed in the context of the following important U.S. regional concerns:

- Strategic relations between the United States and Russia, specifically arms control;
- The impact of a change from the status quo on European security, specifically NATO relations;
- The impact of change from the status quo on U.S. allies in East Asia, where a U.S. deployment of IRBMs would be most likely in response to China's modernization efforts; and
- The impact of a change in U.S. policy on larger nonproliferation goals and its support for critical nonproliferation regimes and initiatives.

Step 4. Define potential ways forward

Building upon the discussion of potential political and military costs of a shift from the status quo, the study attempts to devise and explain potential ways forward that will address U.S. national security interests and address the potential threats of missile proliferation.

Figure 1.1
Analytical Structure of this Study

Evaluate trends in missile proliferation	Assess key INF missile threats to U.S. interests	Analyze likely costs of INF Treaty withdrawal	Define policy implications and potential ways forward
	What are specific regional missile threats?	Are U.S. IRBMs necessary to deter adversaries?	Do military benefits outweigh potential costs?

RAND *MG1181-1.1*

Plan of the Study

The paper is organized as follows:

- Chapter 2 briefly revisits the major components of the INF Treaty, and considers the problem of intermediate-range missile proliferation over the past decade as well as the policies and regimes that have been implemented to restrain it.
- Chapter 3 examines the growing threat of intermediate-range missiles in the arsenals of Iran and North Korea, and considers the ability of the United States to effectively respond to these threats, and whether a new land-based intermediate-range missile is required. The expansion of India and Pakistan's missile forces also will be discussed.
- Chapter 4 focuses on the threat presented by China's missile modernization and the challenges it presents for the United States in responding to a conflict over Taiwan, as well as the potential role of U.S. land-based intermediate-range, conventionally armed missiles in addressing those challenges. It also considers alternative measures available to U.S. policymakers that may be more effective in terms of cost, operational flexibility, and implications for crisis stability.
- Chapter 5 examines the political and security costs of a U.S. withdrawal or cooperative dissolution of the INF.

- Chapter 6 considers potential ways forward, with a focus on expanding the Treaty in the longer term, while maintaining the status quo and addressing the problem of China's modernization through alternative means in the short term.

CHAPTER TWO

Recent History of Missile Proliferation

The proliferation of ballistic and cruise missiles confronts the United States with a significant threat to its national security interests. Since the early- to mid-1960s, Americans have lived with the threat of intercontinental ballistic missiles capable of striking targets within the continental United States. With the end of the Cold War and the achievement of various strategic arms-control agreements with the Soviet Union and its successor states (most importantly Russia), this direct threat to U.S. national security has significantly declined over the past two decades.[1] However, during the same period, the emergence of land-based medium- and intermediate-range ballistic and cruise missiles, whether armed with conventional warheads or potentially with weapons of mass destruction (WMD), in the arsenals of key regional powers increasingly threaten U.S. forces deployed abroad, as well as regional allies. Because of the 1987 INF Treaty, the United States is prohibited from developing or deploying these weapon systems. This study examines the threat posed by land-based intermediate-range missiles in critical regional security contexts. It also assesses the perceived need for the United States to develop and deploy similar missile programs in order to effectively respond to these growing threats. To do so, the United States would need to consider withdrawing from the INF Treaty, which could have significant political and security implications. This chapter will examine the recent history of missile proliferation and present an overview of current proliferation trends. Before

---

[1] Peter Baker, "Senate Passes Arms Control Treaty with Russia, 71-26," *New York Times,* December 22, 2010.

turning to the nature of the new missile challenge to U.S. security, this chapter will briefly revisit the history of the INF Treaty to provide a background for subsequent discussions.

Overview of the INF Treaty

On December 8, 1987, President Ronald Reagan and Soviet General Secretary Mikhail Gorbachev signed the Intermediate Nuclear Forces (INF) Treaty in Washington, D.C. The Treaty—formally titled the *Treaty on the Elimination of Intermediate-Range and Shorter-Range Missiles*—represented a major diplomatic achievement and signified the beginning of a transformation of the relationship between the United States and Soviet Union.[2] Under the requirements of the Treaty, an entire class of weapons was to be eliminated from the arsenals of both superpowers, marking the first time that a strategic arms control agreement actually removed weapons systems rather than instituted numerical limits. Longer- (1,000-5,500 kilometers) and shorter-range (500-1,000 kilometers) land-based missiles—both nuclear and conventionally armed—were covered under the Treaty obligations. That led to the destruction of 2,692 missiles, along with their launchers, equipment, and support and basing facilities. Two formidable opposing intermediate-range ballistic missile systems, the U.S. Pershing II and the Soviet SS-20 as well as ground-launched cruise missiles (GLCMs—most notably the American nuclear-armed BGM-109G Gryphon cruise missile—were removed from Europe and scrapped. These land-based theater nuclear forces (TNF), which had been the source of controversy and domestic political turmoil across Western Europe because of the likelihood that they could be used in a European-wide nuclear conflict, were removed. Central strategic systems such as air- and submarine-launched systems and ICBMs were left to be addressed by the Strategic Arms Reduction Treaty (START).[3] A comprehensive Elimination Pro-

---

[2] The full text of the INF Treaty is reproduced in Appendix A.

[3] Strobe Talbott, *Deadly Gambit: The Reagan Administration and the Stalemate in Nuclear Arms Control,* New York: Alfred A. Knopf, 1984.

tocol established specific procedures for destruction so that the recon-
stitution of these missile forces would be effectively impossible without
detection. A production and test flight ban would prevent the development of new forces to replace those destroyed. To implement the treaty,
the superpowers agreed to an extensive program of on-site inspections
and the establishment of a Special Verification Commission to resolve
potential compliance problems. Thus the treaty was both straightforward and comprehensive. It essentially codified a bargain of "global
double-zero," which had been under consideration for years, vitiat-
ing problems of systems located in the eastern Soviet Union or in the
continental United States, and of both warheads and delivery systems,
preventing a race in conventional missile systems after nuclear-armed
systems had been prohibited.[4]

Figure 2.1
The INF Treaty at a Glance

- Signed in 1987 by the United States and Soviet Union/Russia (and successor states)
- Eliminated land-based ballistic and cruise missiles of ranges (nuclear and conventional) of 500–5,500 km
- Resulted in destruction of 2,692 missiles, plus launchers and support systems
- Banned testing, development and production of systems
- Implemented with intrusive on-sight inspection regime
- Either signatory can withdraw with six months notification, including a statement explaining "extraordinary events… jeopardizing its supreme interests."

RAND *MG1181-2.1*

---

[4] On the history of the negotiations, see Maynard W. Glitman, *The Last Battle of the Cold War: An Inside Account of Negotiating the Intermediate Range Nuclear Forces Treaty*, New York: Palgrave Macmillan, 2006; George L. Rueckert, *Global Double Zero: The INF Treaty from Its Origins to Implementation*, Westport: Greenwood Press, 1993.

Several key points are worth emphasizing for the purposes of the subsequent discussion and analysis of this study. First, precisely because of the difficulty of verification of a class of weapons that would most likely be deployed on mobile launchers and typically concealed or dispersed in ways to avoid detection, in signing the INF Treaty the United States and Soviet Union adopted significant measures to decrease the potential for cheating.[5] Moreover, the development and production of these systems would prove challenging for prevailing national technical means of verification, as opposed to larger silo-based ICBMs, submarines and SLBMs, and strategic bomber forces. Thus, a significant portion of the Treaty and the accompanying Memoranda of Understanding (MOUs) set out the obligations of each party in explicit detail.[6] Ultimately, the challenges of verification made the distinction between nuclear-armed and conventional missiles impossible to address in any credible fashion, leading to the comprehensive agreement to destroy existing systems under intrusive supervision and the banning of any and all testing, development, and production of subsequent systems that would fall under the definition of Intermediate-Range Nuclear Forces.[7]

Finally, the United States and Soviet Union agreed that the INF Treaty would be of unlimited duration. It has no expiration date, and thus remains in effect. With the breakup of the Soviet Union, the INF Treaty devolved to cover the successor states, including Russia, Ukraine, Belarus, Kazakhstan, Turkmenistan, and Uzbekistan. The signatories agreed that either state could withdraw from the Treaty with six months' notice. But to do so, the withdrawing party would have to provide a formal rationale for its decision, specifying the "extraordinary events the notifying Party regards as having jeopardized its supreme interests." Thus, for either the United States or Russia to withdraw, a public case must be presented for doing so. This obligation, defined in

---

[5] The Elimination and Inspection Protocols can be viewed at http://www.state.gov/t/avc/trty/102360.htm#text

[6] The Memoranda of Understanding can be viewed at http://www.state.gov/t/avc/trty/102360.htm#mou

[7] Rueckert, 1993, p. 80.

Article XV of the Treaty, confronts both states with a significant diplomatic challenge, precisely because the withdrawing party would be pressed to name the source of the threat(s) it faces.

Recent Developments

In October 2007, Russian President Vladimir Putin publicly warned the United States that Russia would consider withdrawing from the INF Treaty. Putin raised the issue prior to talks with then-Secretary of Defense Robert Gates and then-Secretary of State Condoleezza Rice in Moscow.[8] While this was Moscow's first official public threat to withdraw from the Treaty, Russian Defense Minister Sergei Ivanov reportedly broached the possibility of Russia's withdrawal in meetings with then-U.S. Secretary of Defense Donald Rumsfeld in March 2005.[9] The Russian foreign ministry reportedly reassured the Bush administration that Russia remained committed to the Treaty soon after these private discussions, but the issue of withdrawal has received significant attention in Russian policy circles.[10] In both cases, the Russian threats were widely interpreted as a response to U.S. plans for ballistic missile defense installations in Central Europe. Putin's suggestion of a Russian withdrawal from the INF Treaty was considered to be influenced by the Bush administration's decision to withdraw from the Anti-Ballistic Missile (ABM) Treaty in 2002 and the subsequent announcement of plans to deploy missile defense facilities in Poland and the Czech Republic.[11] The threat of INF withdrawal, and the formal July 2007 suspension of Russian compliance with the Conventional Forces

---

[8] Luke Harding, "Putin Threatens Withdrawal from Cold War Treaty," *Guardian*, October 12, 2007.

[9] Guy Dinmore, Demetri Sevastopulo, and Hubert Wetzel, "Russia Confronted Rumsfeld with Threat to Quit Treaty," *Financial Times*, March 9, 2005.

[10] Nikolai Khorunzhiy, "Should Russia Quit Treaty on Medium- and Short-Range Missiles?" *RIA Novosti* (On-Line), November 4, 2007; Andrei Kislyakov, "A Bad Treaty Is Better Than a Good Missile," *McClatchy-Tribune News Service*, February 21, 2007.

[11] Anatoli Diakov and Frank von Hippel, *Challenges and Opportunities for Russia-U.S. Nuclear Arms Control*, Washington: The Century Foundation, 2009, pp. 20–21.

Europe (CFE) Treaty, was viewed as a response to the U.S. plans to move forward with its ballistic missile defense (BMD) plans without adequate accommodation for Russian concerns.[12]

A component of Russia's elite perceives U.S. BMD plans for Europe as a potential threat to Russia's nuclear deterrent force.[13] While both the Bush and Obama administrations have attempted to reassure Moscow that Iran is the primary target of the any eventual operational system, Russia remains skeptical. The Obama administration has decided to deploy the "Phased Adaptive Approach," which when completed is expected to provide coverage against an Iranian intermediate-range missile capability in a shorter period of time. By initially utilizing more mature technologies incorporated in the existing sea-based Aegis missile defense system, the administration's decision explicitly embraced this logic.[14] The United States and NATO have further discussed the potential for cooperation with Russia on missile defense in the future, but little progress has been made in assuaging Russian concerns.[15] However, with no guarantees that the system will indeed be limited in scope or an effective "veto" or concrete structure of "joint control" in the offing, Russia is likely to continue to view the system as a potential threat. The potential for expansion of the European missile defense system over time is particularly troubling to Russia, as its strategic forces decline in quantitative terms due to attrition and adherence to arms control agreements such as the "New START" Treaty.[16]

---

[12] Luke Harding, "Kremlin Tears up Arms Pact with NATO: Russia's Relations with West Hit a New Low Point," *The Observer* (On-line), July 14, 2007; Andrew E. Kramer and Thom Shanker, "Russia Steps Back from Key Arms Treaty," *New York Times,* July 14, 2007.

[13] "Russia Would Benefit from Leaving INF Treaty, Say Analysts," *BBC Worldwide Monitoring,* February 15, 2007.

[14] Steven A. Hildreth and Carl Eck, "Long-Range Ballistic Missile Defense in Europe," Washington: Congressional Research Service, 2009; Dean A. Wilkening, "Does Missile Defense in Europe Threaten Russia?" *Survival,* Vol. 54, No. 1, 2012.

[15] Simon Shuster, "Russia Wants a Finger on Europe's Nuclear Shield," *Time (Online),* March 25, 2011.

[16] Alexei Arbatov, *Gambit or Endgame? The New State of Arms Control,* Washington: Carnegie Endowment for International Peace, 2011.

Nonetheless, there is no direct or formal linkage between Moscow's threats to withdraw from the INF Treaty and U.S. ballistic missile defense deployments. Even more expansive missile defense plans that would utilize a ground-based interceptor (GBI, which would have been deployed in Poland under the Bush plan) would not constitute a technical violation of the INF Treaty.[17] While the GBI planned for deployment could ostensibly possess technical characteristics and capabilities similar to that of an intermediate-range ballistic missile, the INF Treaty explicitly addresses this potential problem. Article VII, Section 3 is unambiguous on this matter:

> If a GLBM is of a type developed and tested solely to intercept and counter objects not located on the surface of the earth, it shall not be considered to be a missile to which the limitations of this Treaty apply.[18]

Thus, so long as the interceptors are deployed in their planned defensive, anti-missile role, there is no inherent problem with U.S. BMD plans insofar as the INF Treaty is concerned.

More important, perhaps, is that the ensuing debate among defense and foreign policy elites seemed to conclude that Russia does not require INF missiles to effectively address any perceived threat created by an operational U.S.-NATO BMD system.[19] Shorter range missiles such as the Iskander-M, a highly accurate, stealthy missile with a range of approximately 350 km, is more than adequate to threaten interceptor bases in Poland from a deployment in Kaliningrad or elsewhere—as Putin and Medvedev both threatened on occasion.[20]

---

[17] F. Stephen Larrabee, "Whither Missile Defense?" *International Spectator,* Vol. 43, No. 2, 2008.

[18] See the INF Treaty reproduced in Appendix A. For discussion, see Alexei Arbatov, "Missile Defense and the Intermediate Nuclear Forces Treaty," International Commission on Nuclear Non-proliferation and Disarmament, March 2009.

[19] "No Need for Medium-Range Missiles in Russia's Western Regions—Defence Ministry," *BBC Worldwide Monitoring,* July 18, 2007.

[20] Kevin Flynn, "Medvedev Delivers Chilling Words on Missile Plans," *Independent,* November 5, 2008; "Russia 'May Deploy Missiles in Belarus'," *Turkish Daily News,* November 15, 2007.

Moreover, given the geography of Central Europe, it is highly likely that air-launched cruise missiles would be capable of hitting targets associated with the missile defense systems, such as radar installations in the Czech Republic, Rumania, or perhaps, over time, Turkey.[21]

Ultimately, the Russian threats to withdraw from the INF Treaty seem more influenced by domestic politics and diplomacy. Russian observers have presented the threat of INF withdrawal as a very public reassertion of Russia's prerogative as a great power to protect its interests in a way similar to that of the United States in its withdrawal from the ABM Treaty. This effort plays to both domestic and foreign audiences.[22] Considering Russia's expansive geography, claims of INF missile threats from countries such as China, Iran, India, Pakistan, and North Korea are legitimate, but traditional deterrence and diplomatic relations are viewed as being sufficient in addressing them without a resort to costly and technically challenging missile defenses in the views of most Russian commentators.[23] However, the 2007 episode and the subsequent discussions and debates within and among Russian military and foreign policy elites seemed to conclude that on balance, the INF Treaty continued to serve Russian interests, though expansion of the treaty to include those states would greatly enhance its security.[24] If such expansion failed, and if U.S. behavior in the future was deemed provocative—particularly with consideration to the expansion of missile defenses—it should be expected that the threat of INF withdrawal would be revisited.

It is thus not surprising that Russia introduced a resolution at the Conference on Disarmament at the United Nations in October

---

[21] Arbatov, 2009, p. 7.

[22] "TV Commentator Urges Russia's Withdrawal from INF Treaty," *BBC Worldwide Monitoring*, April 2, 2007; "Russia and Arms Control: Vlad and MAD," *The Economist*, June 7, 2007.

[23] Arbatov, 2011, pp. 18–19.

[24] Arbatov, 2009, pp. 8–10; "INF Treaty Pullout May Lead to New Arms Race—Russian General," *BBC Worldwide Monitoring*, February 19, 2007; Kislyakov, 2007.

2007 to "globalize" or multi-lateralize the INF Treaty.[25] The United States supported the resolution and has continued to formally express its approval, but little real diplomatic progress has been made.[26] The kind of deep cooperation with Russia necessary to leverage the two nations' concerns about INF missiles has not emerged, nor has the exploration of the potential willingness of countries such as China to engage in such a process.

Trends in Ballistic Missile Proliferation After the Cold War

Missile proliferation has been a central concern of U.S. policymakers since the end of the Cold War. The spread of missiles and their component technologies around the globe increased the threat that the United States or its allies could be attacked with WMD. Regional powers suspected of maintaining programs in biological, chemical, or radiological weapons and perhaps actively seeking nuclear weapons seemed intent on acquiring and developing missile capabilities to deliver these weapons. First Russian- and eventually Chinese-made SCUD missiles emerged in the arsenals of a variety of regional powers. SCUD-B missiles, for example, with a range of approximately 300 km, could be found in Afghanistan, Armenia, Belarus, Egypt, Georgia, Iran, Kazakhstan, Libya, North Korea, Romania, Syria, Turkmenistan, UAE, Vietnam, and Yemen. Similarly, SCUD-C missiles, with an approximate range of 500 km, could be found in numbers in regional powers like North Korea, Iran, and Syria.[27]

In small numbers, these weapons provide limited military utility. But their increasing prevalence reflected the perceived political and prestige benefits to smaller regional militaries. For these states, ballis-

---

[25] Vladimir Petrov, "Russia Releases Draft of Global INF Treaty," *Jane's Defence Weekly*, February 22, 2008; "Russian Defence Ministry Marks INF Treaty Anniversary, Backs Globalization," *BBC Worldwide Monitoring*, June 4, 2008.

[26] Vladimir Petrov, "Russia, US Issue Call for Widening of INF Treaty," *Jane's Defence Weekly*, November 7, 2007.

[27] "Russia 'May Deploy Missiles in Belarus,'" 2007.

tic missiles serve as a relatively cost-effective deterrent to the superior conventional military power of the United States or its regional allies.[28] In the case of North Korea and Iran, these shorter-range ballistic missile systems also have served as the basis for the development indigenous longer-range missiles. As the 2001 National Intelligence Estimate reflects:

> Nevertheless, the missile threat will continue to grow, in part because missiles have become important regional weapons in the

Table 2.1
Global SCUD B, C, and D Inventories

Program		
SCUD-B	**SCUD-C**	**SCUD-D**
Afghanistan	Egypt	Syria
Armenia	Iran	
Belarus	DPRK	
Egypt	Syria	
Georgia	Yemen	
Iran		
Kazakhstan		
Libya		
DPRK		
Romania		
Russia		
Syria		
Turkmenistan		
Ukrain		
UAE		
Vietnam		
Yemen		

SOURCE: "Fact Sheet: The Missile Technology Control Regime at a Glance," Arms Control Association, August 2012.

---

[28] John R. Harvey, "Ballistic Missiles and Advanced Strike Aircraft: Comparing Military Effectiveness," *International Security*, Vol. 17, No. 2, 1992.

arsenals of numerous countries. Moreover, missiles provide a level of prestige, coercive diplomacy, and deterrence that non-missile means do not.[29]

The United States and its partners have had some significant successes in limiting the proliferation of missiles in the past two decades. Despite more pessimistic analyses that drove the U.S. political debate concerning national missile defenses in the late 1990s, horizontal proliferation—the spread of new missile programs—has remained relatively limited.[30] First, the MTCR emerged as a voluntary agreement among participating states to prevent the export of critical components for missile development. Founded in 1987 by the United States, the United Kingdom, Canada, France, Germany, Italy, and Japan, the MTCR has increased its membership to include 34 members, perhaps most importantly Russia, which formally joined in 1995. Many of the former Warsaw Pact nations, which possessed capabilities to develop and export missiles and relevant technologies, joined in the late 1990s and 2000s.[31] The MTCR sets out two categories of items that signatories are expected to address in the export control policies:

> Category I includes complete missiles and rockets, major sub-systems and production facilities. Specialized materials, technologies, propellants, sub-components for missiles and rockets comprise Category II.[32]

---

[29] National Intelligence Council, *Foreign Missile Development and the Ballistic Missile Threat Through 2015*, Washington, 2001, p. 7.

[30] "Final Report," The Commission to Assess the Ballistic Missile Threat to the United States, July 15, 1998.

[31] On the development of the MTCR, see Dinshaw Mistry, *Containing Missile Proliferation: Strategic Technology, Security Regimes, and International Cooperation in Arms Control,* Seattle: University of Washington Press, 2003; Deborah A. Ozga, "A Chronology of the Missile Technology Control Regime," *Nonproliferation Review,* Winter 1994; Wyn Bowen, "U.S. Policy on Ballistic Missile Proliferation: The MTCR's First Decade (1987-1997)," *Nonproliferation Review,* 1997.

[32] "Fact Sheet: The Missile Technology Control Regime at a Glance," Washington: Arms Control Association.

While it remains a voluntary organization, MTCR members agree to employ "a strong presumption to deny" any Category I transfers when considering possible exports. Because of the potential civilian applications of many Category II items, members are urged to exercise caution in any export decisions, but fewer restrictions apply. Ultimately, members are expected to consider the likely motives and intentions of the state requesting transfers, particularly with regard to acquisition of WMD. Initially focusing on missiles as potential delivery vehicles for WMD, and particularly nuclear warheads, the MTCR initially set a ceiling of 300km range/500 kg payload for exportable missiles. While this guideline would realistically limit most SCUD-type systems, concerns emerged that it could allow for other WMD-equipped warheads.[33] For example, chemical or biological weapons would not require a warhead in excess of 500 kg. Moreover, while cruise missiles are formally covered under the MTCR, the range/payload guideline effectively provided an opening for significant cruise missile proliferation.[34] At the time of the MTCR's founding, the technology associated with advance cruise missiles, such as those in the superpower arsenals, was generally perceived as beyond the technical capacity of likely proliferators.[35] This is no longer the case, and cruise missile systems have emerged and expanded over the past decade. The challenge of cruise missiles will be discussed further below.

One major power that has remained outside of the MTCR is China. Concerns persisted about China's proliferation activities throughout the 1980s. However, China agreed to abide by the MTCR's guidelines in 1992, after negotiations with the United States to lift sanctions on Chinese firms, but subsequently refused to adhere to updated guidelines set forth in 1993 when the regime expanded its prohibitions to cover all WMD-capable missiles, not just

---

[33] Waheguru Pal Singh Sidhu, "Looking Back: The Missile Technology Control Regime," *Arms Control Today,* April 2007.

[34] Dennis M. Gormley, *Missile Contagion: Cruise Missile Proliferation and the Threat to International Security,* Annapolis: Naval Institute Press, 2008, pp. 151–52.

[35] Sidhu, 2007.

Table 2.2
MTCR Members

Partner	Year Joined	Partner	Year Joined	Partner	Year Joined
Argentina	1993	Greece	1992	Republic of Korea	2001
Australia	1990	Hungary	1993	Russian Federation	1995
Austria	1991	Iceland	1993	South Africa	1995
Belgium	1990	Ireland	1992	Spain	1990
Brazil	1995	Italy	1987	Sweden	1991
Bulgaria	2004	Japan	1987	Switzerland	1992
Canada	1987	Luxembourg	1990	Turkey	1997
Czech Republic	1998	Netherlands	1990	Ukraine	1998
Denmark	1990	New Zealand	1991	United Kingdom	1987
Finland	1991	Norway	1990	United States of America	1987
France	1987	Poland	1998		
Germany	1987	Portugal	1992		

SOURCE: Website of the Missile Technology Control Regime, accessed at http://www.mtcr.info/english/index.html.

nuclear.[36] China offered to formally join the regime in 2004, but has not become a formal member due to persistent concerns about Beijing's perceived willingness to cooperate with Pakistan and Iran.[37] Observers contend that Beijing has significantly tightened its export control policies during the period, but challenges remain to implementing rigorous export controls.[38]

More broadly, under bilateral U.S. pressures, and additional voluntary multilateral diplomatic arrangements such as the PSI, general or horizontal proliferation trends have declined over the past two decades, primarily limited to states outside of the MTCR. Obtaining complete missile systems and necessary critical component technologies has become significantly more difficult as these supply-side-oriented instruments have expanded over time. Moreover, the inability of states that may seek missile technology to gain access to outside technical expertise and assistance has provided a further barrier to entry. Such technical assistance has been deemed to be critical to the development of regional programs.[39]

For example, the constraints implemented on export controls under the MTCR and other national and multilateral sanctions regimes seem to have significantly hindered both the Iranian and North Korean ballistic missile programs. Without the critical access to technical assistance, as well as component technologies and systems, it has been difficult for Iran to make significant progress over the past decade. In the absence of the MTCR and the international cooperation to limit the proliferation of missiles and missile technologies, it would seem that both of these states would be much further along in the development

---

[36] Andrew Feickert, "Missile Technology Control Regime (MTCR) and International Code of Conduct against Ballistic Missile Proliferation (ICOC): Background and Issues for Congress," Washington: Congressional Research Service, April 8, 2003, p. 5; Sidhu, 2007.

[37] Gormley, 2008, pp. 61–62.

[38] Shirley A. Kan, *China and Proliferation of Weapons of Mass Destruction and Missiles: Policy Issues,* Washington: Congressional Research Service, 2011; Evan S. Medeiros, *Chasing the Dragon: Assessing China's Export Controls for WMD-Related Goods and Technologies,* Santa Monica, Calif.: RAND Corporation, MG-353, 2005.

[39] National Intelligence Council, 2001; "Iran's Nuclear and Missile Potential: A Joint Threat Assessment by U.S. and Russian Technical Experts," New York: East West Institute, 2009.

of longer-range missile programs. As one prominent panel of experts has concluded:

> The Rumsfeld Commission Report on the ballistic missile threat to the United States assumed that the newly-emerging missile states could achieve significant ballistic missile capability quickly by using the experience—and avoiding the mistakes—of the traditional missile states. This assumption is not supported by developments since the Commission published its report in 1998. This is probably because the Commission failed to give adequate weight to the enormous diversity and complexity of the specialized technical problems associated with each of the seemingly simple and small steps in the development of ballistic missiles.... Without direct foreign assistance, new missile states must, on their own, simultaneously address and solve numerous problems and overcome many obstacles during each stage of the development process.[40]

Beyond the MTCR, during the 1990s, the United States engaged in a multi-faceted approach to more effectively address the problem of proliferation of missiles and WMD.[41] The George H. W. Bush administration enacted the Enhanced Proliferation Control Initiative (EPCI) in December 1990, which tightened export controls and required American companies to acquire licenses for missile- and WMD-related technologies. Following on this, the United States engaged in bilateral negotiations with the Soviet Union/Russia to adhere to MTCR guidelines and eventually have it formally join the regime in 1995. Similarly, intensive discussions with China to curtail the export of missile technologies in return for lifting sanctions against Chinese firms culminated in China's formal pledge to follow MTCR guidelines. At the same time, the United States worked closely with countries such as Germany and Italy on harmonizing their export control policies.[42]

---

[40] Ibid., p. 10.

[41] Feickert, 2003.

[42] Bowen, 1997.

In the late 1990s, because of perceived limitations of the supply-side nature of the MTCR, members of the regime began to examine means to more comprehensively address the challenge of missile proliferation by developing a code of conduct that could be extended to non-MTCR members. The International Code of Conduct Against Ballistic Missile Proliferation (the ICOC or "The Hague Code") was introduced in 2002, with 93 countries initially signing on. As of 2008, 124 countries had signed the Code.[43] However, with its focus on confidence-building measures and efforts to enhance transparency, such as "annual declarations of their ballistic missile policies and launches, as well as SLV policy, inventories, and launches," the impact of the ICOC has been limited thus far.[44] Moreover, countries such as Syria, North Korea, Iraq, China, Pakistan, India, and Israel have not signed the Code.

Finally, the PSI is an informal voluntary cooperative initiative composed of states that agree to take collective action against the trafficking of weapons of mass destruction and delivery systems among states and non-state actors. It was introduced by the George W. Bush administration in May 2003 and currently has 90 participants who commit to:

> ... interdict transfers to and from states and non-state actors of proliferation concern to the extent of their capabilities and legal authorities; develop procedures to facilitate exchange of information with other countries; strengthen national legal authorities to facilitate interdiction; and take specific actions in support of interdiction efforts.[45]

PSI efforts have largely focused on developing protocols and agreements for stopping, boarding, and (if necessary) seizing ships at sea suspected of transporting WMD, missile technologies, or related materials. The program has created some controversy. Most notably,

---

[43] Gormley, 2008.

[44] Feickert, 2003, p. 12.

[45] United States Department of State, "Proliferation Security Initiative."

while claims of successful interdictions under PSI auspices have been made, it is less clear that the activities in question were indeed related to the initiative or executed under other mandates, such as UN resolutions.[46] Moreover, the informality and ad hoc nature of the initiative seemingly has undermined its attraction in the views of some states that would prefer a more formal, legal approach.[47] Nonetheless, with an increasing membership, the PSI provides a potential deterrent to states or non-state actors seeking to transfer illicit technologies.[48]

International nonproliferation efforts have been less successful in the realm of restraining *vertical* proliferation, or the enhancement of existing missile programs within states that have achieved some level of indigenous missile production capacity or stockpiles of imported weapons. With domestic political support, financial resources, and technical and industrial capacity to reverse-engineer and leverage technologies of imported weapons and the ostensible security threats to drive further acquisition and development programs, a relatively small number of states have increased their missile capabilities during the past decade. Specifically, a number of states have engaged in the development of land-based intermediate-range ballistic and cruise missiles, those proscribed by the 1987 INF Treaty and removed from the arsenals of the United States and Russia. The most acute threats have emerged from states with growing missile capabilities combined with existing or potential WMD programs. Since 2001, this problem of vertical proliferation in the context of several key regional contexts has characterized a critical challenge to U.S. security interests, as a National Intelligence Council report explained:

> The trend in ballistic missile development worldwide is toward a maturation process among existing ballistic missile programs rather than toward a large increase in the number of countries

---

[46] Wade Boese, "Interdiction Initiative Successes Assessed," *Arms Control Today*, June/August 2008.

[47] Mark J. Valencia, "The Proliferation Security Initiative: A Glass Half-Full," *Arms Control Today*, June 2007.

[48] Boese, 2008; Valencia, 2007.

processing ballistic missiles. Emerging ballistic missile states continue to increase the range, reliability, and accuracy of the missile systems in their inventories—posing ever greater risks to US
forces, interests, and allies through the world.[49]

Several regional powers now possess land-based missile capabilities
that challenge U.S. security interests. North Korea's persistence in
acquiring a missile capability in support of its nuclear weapons program poses a threat to U.S. allies and possibly to the United States
itself. Iran's progress toward a nuclear weapon has intensified rivalries
in the Middle East, and an eventual nuclear missile capability presents
a potential threat beyond the region, as well as the increased likelihood
of further proliferation in the region. Both India and Pakistan have
invested in the development of these missile systems in their growing
strategic rivalry, with implications beyond the Indian Subcontinent.
Finally, China has developed a robust arsenal of short- and medium-
range conventionally-armed ballistic and cruise missiles that threaten
Taiwan and also present significant challenges to the United States in
effectively responding to Taiwan's defense in the event of a crisis.

The Problem of Cruise Missile Proliferation

One area in which non-proliferation efforts have had little success is
in addressing the spread of cruise missiles. As security expert Dennis
Gormley has persuasively argued, a major oversight of both the MTCR
and the ICOC is the failure to adequately address the growing problem
of land attack cruise missile (LACM) proliferation.[50] While ballistic
missile proliferation has been slowed over the past two decades, cruise
missile programs have increased and expanded around the globe. Several important regional powers have focused on the development and
deployment of land-based intermediate-range cruise missiles. LACMs

---

[49] National Intelligence Council, 2001, p. 5.

[50] Gormley, 2008; Dennis M. Gormley, "Winning on Ballistic Missiles but Losing on
Cruise: The Missile Proliferation Battle," *Arms Control Today*, December 2009.

Table 2.3
Key Global INF Missile Inventories

Country	System	Range (km)	Payload (kg)
China	DF-3A/CSS-2	2800	2150
	DF-15/CSS-6	600	500
	DF-21/CSS-5.1	2500	600
	DF-21A/CSS-5.2	1770+	2000
DPRK	No-Dong-2	1500	770
	Taepo-Dong-1	2000	1000
	Taepo-Dong-2	3500-5500	1000
Iran	Shahab 3	800-1300	1200
	Shahab 3+	1500-2500	800
India	Agni-2	2000	1000
	Agni-3	3000	1000
Pakistan	Ghauri-2	2300	700
	Shaheen-2	2500	1000
Israel	Jericho-2	1500	1000
	Jericho-3	3000-6500	1000

SOURCE: "Fact Sheet: Worldwide Ballistic Missile Inventories," Arms Control Association, January 2012.

have emerged as a highly-valued system, having been influenced by the major role that the Tomahawk cruise missile has played in U.S. military operations in Iraq and elsewhere during the 1990s and other important factors that make cruise missiles particularly attractive

Operationally, LACMs appeared to trump ballistic missiles in accuracy (by at least a factor of ten), cost (cheaper by a factor of two or more), ease of operations and maintenance, greater mobil-

ity for ground-launched versions (making them less susceptible to
counterforce strikes), aerodynamic stability...[51]

Moreover, while ballistic missile defenses have proven increasingly capable of detecting and intercepting ballistic missiles, no such
defenses against cruise missiles have been developed. Notably, during
the 2003 Iraq war, the United States was able to shoot down nine
Iraqi ballistic missiles but failed to destroy five rather primitive cruise
missiles.[52] This inability to defend against cruise missiles only adds to
their perceived value to regional powers. For example, the significant
expansion of China's intermediate range missiles has, in fact, been due
primarily to the production of the DH-10 over the past three years.
The Babur/Hatf-7 land-based intermediate-range cruise missile has
been publicly portrayed as a vital component of Pakistan's nuclear
deterrent in response to India's initial moves to develop and deploy
missile defenses precisely because of its high likelihood of penetrating any such defenses. In response, India has built upon the Brah-
mos short-range cruise missile, which it jointly developed with Russia,
to develop the Nirhbay land-based intermediate-range cruise missile.
South Korea, which the United States has pushed away from development of ballistic missiles, is believed to have four different land-based
intermediate-range cruise missile programs under development. Taiwan
has reportedly made significant progress toward the development of an
intermediate-range LACM that could hit targets well into mainland
China.[53] The INF Treaty would proscribe all of these programs if these
countries were members.

The MTCR had initially included cruise missiles and unmanned
aerial vehicles, and has since updated its guidelines to better address
the proliferation of these systems.[54] However, because many of the
technical components of cruise missiles also are used in aircraft and

---

[51] Ibid., pp. 107–08.

[52] Ibid., pp. 51, 108.

[53] The preceding cruise missile programs and specifications can be found in Appendix A,
"Selected Cruise Missile Programs," in Gormley, 2008; Ibid., pp. 178–80.

[54] Ibid., pp. 134–35.

other civilian applications, the ability to acquire them is much less difficult.[55] The inherently dual-use nature of cruise missile technology presents a major challenge for export control regimes.[56] Moreover, the initial range/payload limitations prohibited under the MTCR left open the potential to build and export fairly robust cruise missile programs and "the letters" of the guidelines have been used to skirt what some would consider "the spirit" of the regime even by generally committed members.[57] Less explicably, the ICOC failed to address cruise missiles in its attempt to develop norms for possessing ballistic missiles, creating what some see as an uneven emphasis on the perceived dangers of the proliferation of the two weapons.[58]

The proliferation of advanced land-based intermediate-range cruise missile programs has allowed states to expand their capabilities in a relatively short time. These systems, which are perceived to possess greater accuracy and penetrability than ballistic missiles, at a much lower per unit cost, are also typically smaller and more difficult to locate and track. When armed with nuclear weapons, they can thus provide a robust, second-strike capability, but their presence can also intensify fears of a first strike in the event of a diplomatic crisis. The emergence of these systems, and their attractiveness to developing militaries, confronts the United States and its allies in the cause of missile nonproliferation with a significant challenge.

While the problem of missile proliferation has certainly not been solved, the MTCR and the concurrent harmonization of export controls in many of the advanced nations have had a positive impact of reducing horizontal proliferation. The development of a multilateral rule-based International Code of Conduct has, up to this point, made less of a contribution. But over time, the confidence-building measures and norms of appropriate behavior may bolster the larger nonproliferation effort. Finally, the PSI, while ad hoc and informal,

---

[55] Feickert, 2003, p. 11.

[56] Gormley, 2008, p. 7.

[57] Ibid., pp. 151–52.

[58] Ibid., pp. 12–13.

presents would-be proliferators with the prospects of interdiction and exposure, providing a deterrent that supports the norms and rules that have emerged over the past two decades. It is difficult to quantify or clearly demonstrate the strength of these norms, or whether they will persist. However, it seems clear that after two decades, some progress has been made, particularly on the supply-side of proliferation. A U.S. decision to withdraw from or cooperatively dissolve the INF Treaty should be considered against the background of the larger U.S. commitment to nonproliferation and the potential impact such a diplomatic action would have on these cooperative measures over the longer term.

CHAPTER THREE

Emerging Missile Threats Facing the United States

The importance of the emergence of land-based intermediate-range missile programs is most evident in the cases of India, Pakistan, Iran, and North Korea. Intermediate-range missiles provide these states with the capability to project power at the regional level and, with access to nuclear warheads, serve as the central components of nuclear deterrent forces against their regional adversaries or perhaps conventionally superior military powers like the United States. Nonetheless, each of these programs confronts the United States with different challenges. The expansion of capabilities of India and Pakistan, and their respective utilization of intermediate-range missile programs to deliver nuclear weapons, presents problems for the United States, but neither presents a direct threat to U.S. security interests. Conversely, Iran's missile programs currently present a conventional threat to the United States and its allies in the Middle East. But if it were to develop nuclear weapons, the threat would increase significantly.

This chapter will examine the challenges created by these growing intermediate-range missile programs. First, and most directly, the intermediate-range missile programs of Iran and North Korea confront the United States and its Middle East and East Asian allies, respectively. The nature of these threats will be systematically analyzed using a straightforward conceptual framework based on key recent works in the deterrence literature. After outlining the major security interests of these states, the nature of the threat posed by intermediate-range missiles to the United States and its relevant regional allies—now and in the near future—will be assessed. Current U.S. and allied capabilities to address these threats will be evaluated, and the potential contributions of intermediate-range missiles to the U.S. capabilities to effectively deter or, if necessary, defend against these threats will be considered, as will alternatives. Finally, the growing prevalence of intermediate-range missiles in the India-Pakistan rivalry will be assessed, as will its implications for crisis stability and the probability of conflict on the Subcontinent. Given U.S. relations with both states and its engagement in Afghanistan, avoiding crisis and conflict and dampening historic tensions between India and Pakistan is an important concern.

Regional Deterrence: A Framework for Analysis

The framework utilized to assess the potential missile threats of Iran, North Korea, and China and existing and potential U.S. capabilities to effectively deter, or, if necessary, defend against these threats is derived from previous RAND research. Specifically, two recent works—Dean Wilkening and Kenneth Watman's *Nuclear Deterrence in a Regional Context* and David Ochmanek and Lowell Schwartz's *The Challenge of Nuclear-Armed Regional Adversaries*—provide useful guidelines for considering the policies and capabilities required to deter regional powers with nuclear programs.[1] These works engage much of the larger historical deterrence literature and attempt to apply key lessons and concepts to regional contexts.[2] An obvious caveat is that North Korea possesses nuclear weapons, while Iran had not achieved that capabil-

---

[1] Dean Wilkening and Kenneth Watman, *Nuclear Deterrence in a Regional Context,* Santa Monica, Calif.: RAND Corporation, MR-500-A/AF, 1995; David Ochmanek and Lowell H. Schwartz, *The Challenge of Nuclear-Armed Regional Adversaries,* Santa Monica, Calif.: RAND Corporation, MG-671-AF, 2008; Austin Long, *Deterrence -- From Cold War to Long War: Lessons from Six Decades of Rand Research,* Santa Monica, Calif.: RAND Corporation, MG-636-OSD/AF, 2008.

[2] Among key works in the deterrence literature, see Alexander George and Richard Smoke, *Deterrence in American Foreign Policy: Theory and Practice,* New York: Columbia University Press, 1974; Paul K. Huth, *Extended Deterrence and the Prevention of War,* New Haven: Yale University Press, 1988; John J. Mearsheimer, *Conventional Deterrence,* Ithaca: Cornell University Press, 1985; Glenn Snyder, *Deterrence and Defense: Toward a Theory of National Security,* Princeton: Princeton University Press, 1961.

ity as of mid-2012. Moreover, the nature of China's missile threat is primarily conventional in the context of a conflict over Taiwan.[3] At the same time, these works provide a fairly straightforward means of understanding the key elements that contribute to regional deterrence and capture the challenges confronting the United States. A central assumption, particularly applicable to the Iranian and North Korean cases, is that intermediate-range missile forces are central systems of these regional powers, and are likely to be highly valued and perceived as vitally important to their deterrent capabilities. An analogy can be drawn to a small, potentially insecure nuclear force, and we can assume that crisis and conflict dynamics would be broadly similar.

The Wilkening and Watman piece presents an explicit model of deterrence that takes into account the critical components of credibility and capabilities. A key assumption of the model (and incorporated in both studies) is that the United States is likely to face an asymmetry of interests vis-à-vis the state in question, particularly once a crisis ensues.[4] On balance, the survival of the regime will be greater than the interests of the United States in any foreseeable conflict. However, as the authors explain, certain military capabilities can overcome perceived asymmetries of interest, and thus enhance the capacity to deter regional adversaries.[5]

> ... [W]hile there is room for creative diplomacy to buttress the perception of U.S. resolve or commitment, the most effective way to strengthen the credibility of U.S. threats, as well as the consequences associated with these threats, is to influence the opponent's perception of U.S. military capabilities so he becomes convinced the United States can respond effectively if he attacks the U.S. homeland, U.S. forces overseas, or U.S. allies. Thus the approach taken here emphasizes asymmetric U.S. military advan-

---

[3] The discussion of China in the next chapter will also draw heavily on Abram N. Shulsky, *Deterrence Theory and Chinese Behavior,* Santa Monica, Calif.: RAND Corporation, MR-1161-AF, 2000.

[4] Wilkening and Watman, 1995, p. 7.

[5] Ibid., pp. 13–14.

tages to compensate for what frequently may be the opponent's perception of a weak U.S. commitment of resolve.[6]

In most foreseeable cases, the United States will possess "escalation dominance" over its regional adversaries, which is defined as "the situation in which the United States can retaliate to nuclear attack by escalating to the same or higher 'rungs of the escalation ladder,' dominating the war at a higher level of violence."[7] However, because of this overwhelming superiority of capabilities, the problem arises that in a crisis or a conflict, regional adversaries may have incentives to escalate (or threaten escalation) against U.S. forces in the region or U.S. allies to de-escalate the crisis and ensure regime survival once the United States has become involved. Thus, retaliatory capabilities that increase the perceived costs to the regional adversary may be less effective, or conversely may push regional adversaries to "use or lose" their capabilities in a conflict. Putting aside the question of commitment or resolve, which may be less applicable in regional crises that do not threaten the U.S. homeland, the balance of military capabilities can alter the adversary's calculations. Specifically, the four capabilities that are considered most important for addressing regional threats are:

- U.S. nuclear superiority
- Active and passive defenses
- Counterforce—particularly conventional—capabilities
- Accurate and timely intelligence.[8]

In regional contexts, U.S. nuclear superiority is assumed, and adversaries that threaten nuclear use (or perhaps other WMD) against U.S. forces or allies must contemplate the possibility of nuclear retaliation.[9] However, to prevent the use of WMD, an alternative is to focus on raising the risks associated with the adversary's policies. Specifically,

---

[6] Ibid., p. 22.

[7] Ibid., p. 41.

[8] Ibid., p. 39.

[9] Ibid., p. 45.

Table 3.1
Regional Deterrence Framework

	Capabilities	
Commitment[a]	Retaliation / Punishment[b]	Denial
Formal Alliances	Strategic Triad[c] - ICBMs - SLBMs	Conventional Counterforce
Public Statements	- Strategic Bombers	Active and Passive Defenses
Diplomatic Communication	Conventional Retaliation	Intelligence

[a] Credibility of commitment is typically less robust in extended deterrence situations.

[b] Threats of punishment, while raising costs, may be less effective in the event of a crisis or a conflict where regime survival may be in doubt.

[c] U.S. threats to employ strategic weapons are less likely to be credible in a regional deterrence scenario.

if the expected benefits of threatening or using WMD in a conflict are significantly decreased by the prospects of effective U.S. counterforce or damage limitation capabilities, adversaries may have less incentive to consider threats in the first place. However, counterforce and damage limitation capabilities may also increase the risks associated with the adversary's likelihood of escalation.[10] Moving forward, the critical question is whether the United States will field adequate capabilities to deter regional powers as their capabilities may increase. Ochmanek and Schwartz expand on the important role of counterforce capabilities in regional contexts:

> Improved capabilities for persistent surveillance and rapid, pre-cision strike can also be useful. While offensive counterforce cannot be regarded as a panacea, it is worth pursuing improve-ments in capabilities to monitor activities over large areas; hunt down small, mobile targets; and destroy them promptly. Toward this end, better human intelligence, larger numbers of unmanned aerial vehicles, a broader array of sensor systems, improved means

---

[10] Ibid., p. 49.

for automatic target recognition, and loitering "kill" systems (manned or unmanned) would be most relevant.[11]

Working along similar lines as counterforce capabilities, assets that can contribute to decreasing the expected benefits an adversary may achieve, or denial, may also be particularly useful in the regional deterrence context. While threats of escalation (or punishment/raising costs) may be less effective, capabilities that contribute to decrease the likelihood that the adversary can expect to achieve his goals will necessarily affect his calculations. Those capabilities also can enhance the ability of the United States and regional allies to deter an adversary from provocative behavior or escalation in the event of a crisis.[12]

When considering the effectiveness of U.S. existing and likely available capabilities to deter regional threats, it also is important to consider the potential escalatory dynamics that may arise in a crisis or conflict situation precisely because of the often-overwhelming nature of U.S. conventional and nuclear capabilities.[13] Moreover, as mentioned above, while counterforce capabilities may indeed make adversaries less likely to initiate a conflict, these same capabilities may lead them to escalate once a crisis or conflict has begun. Fears that the United States or allies could eliminate the most important components of their arsenals may lead states to consider "using or losing" them before it is too late. In such cases, it is important to know what kinds of targets may cause adversaries to fear that the U.S. is intent on regime change or disarming the adversary, which could less-directly but still significantly endanger regime survival.

More generally, it is difficult to definitively state what capabilities are necessary to effectively deter regional actors. As the history of the conventional and nuclear balance in Europe during the Cold War reflects, the assessment of the relative robustness of deterrence can be

---

[11] Ochmanek and Schwartz, 2008, p. 54.

[12] Wilkening and Watman, 1995, pp. 43–44.

[13] Forrest Morgan, Karl P. Mueller, Evan S. Medeiros, Kevin L. Pollpeter, and Roger Cliff, *Dangerous Thresholds: Managing Escalation in the 21st Century,* Santa Monica, Calif.: RAND Corporation, MG-614-AF, 2008.

an issue of debate.[14] This study is focused on the challenge of missile programs, whether armed with conventional or nuclear warheads, and assumes that the missile forces in question are viewed as central systems in the arsenals of the potential adversaries that the United States may face. Whether because of a perceived lack of alternative conventional power projection capabilities or because of a lack of alternative retaliatory capabilities, medium-range missiles are assumed to be highly valued assets.

In examining the specific regional threats of Iran and North Korea in this chapter and China in the next chapter, this framework will be employed to attempt to assess the capabilities required to maintain or enhance deterrence.

Using this analytical framework, the following questions will be considered in the contexts of the missiles threats posed by Iran, North Korea, and China. While the exact nature of each threat is somewhat different, these questions provide a straightforward means to analyze the threats and potential implications for U.S. policy.

- Does the United States currently possess the capabilities to maintain deterrence in this regional context, given current trends?
- Does the United States require additional capabilities to maintain effective deterrence?
- What role would a new generation of U.S. IRBMs play in maintaining or enhancing U.S. capabilities to deter regional adversaries in the future?

---

[14] Eliot A. Cohen, "Toward Better Net Assessment: Rethinking the European Conventional Balance," *International Security,* Vo. 13, No. 1, 1988; John J. Mearsheimer, "Assessing the Conventional Balance: The 3:1 Rule and Its Critics," *International Security,* Vol. 13, No. 4, 1989; John J. Mearsheimer, Barry R. Posen, and Eliot A. Cohen, "Reassessing Net Assessment," *International Security,* Vol. 13, No. 4, 1989; Barry R. Posen, "Measuring the European Conventional Balance: Coping with Complexity in Threat Assessment," *International Security,* Vol. 9, No. 3, 1984.

The Iranian Missile Threat

Much has been written about the nature of the threat posed by Iran and the regional and global implications of its potential acquisition of nuclear weapons.[15] Given the troubled history between the United States and the Iranian regime; Iran's ongoing support for groups that target Israel; the underlying rivalry between Tehran and other Sunni-Arab states in the Gulf region; and the potential future coupling of nuclear capabilities with a desire to expand its influence, Iran is particularly threatening to U.S. interests. The large and expanding Iranian missile program confronts the United States and its allies with a conventional missile threat in the event of a crisis or conflict. Over time, these missiles may provide Iran with the capacity to deliver nuclear weapons within and beyond the region.[16] The key question is whether the United States possesses the capabilities to effectively address the existing threat of Iran's conventional missiles or whether additional capabilities, including perhaps a deployment of conventional U.S. land-based, intermediate-range ballistic missiles, are necessary to do so. The same question can be applied to a potentially nuclear-armed Iran.

Currently, Iran's missile program plays a vitally important role because it directly addresses three of Tehran's primary security interests: perpetuating the survival of the revolutionary regime, protecting the territorial integrity of Iran, and, where possible, expanding the influence of Iran in the region and perhaps globally.[17] Given its relatively limited conventional capabilities, particularly in the area of strike aircraft, the Iranian missile program improves its conventional capabilities to inflict costs on external powers that would seek to threaten

---

[15] James M. Lindsay and Ray Takeyh, "After Iran Gets the Bomb: Containment and Its Complications," *Foreign Affairs*, Vol. 89, No. 2, 2010; Eric Edelman, Andrew Krepinevich, and Evan Braden Montgomery, "The Dangers of a Nuclear Iran," *Foreign Affairs*, Vol. 90, No. 1, 2011; "Iran's Nuclear and Missile Potential," 2009.

[16] Mark Fitzpatrick, ed., *Iran's Ballistic Missile Capabilities: A Net Assessment*, London: International Institute for Strategic Studies, 2010.

[17] Lynn E. Davis, Jeffrey Martini, Alireza Nader, Dalia Dassa Kaye, James T. Quinlivian, and Paul Steinberg, *Iran's Nuclear Future: Critical U.S. Policy Choices*, Santa Monica, Calif.: RAND Corporation, MG-1087-AF, 2011.

the regime or Iranian territory.[18] With the development of a nuclear capability, Iran's existing land-based intermediate-range missile capabilities provide the regime with a significant enhancement of its ability to deter attacks from regional or global adversaries, and also contribute to a perceived ability to expand its influence in the region. As a recent U.S. intelligence community threat assessment underscores, missiles seem to play a key role in Tehran's planning:

> We judge Iran would likely choose missile delivery as its preferred method of delivering a nuclear weapon. Iran already has the largest inventory of ballistic missiles in the Middle East and it continues to expand the scale, reach and sophistication of its ballistic missile forces—many of which are inherently capable of carrying a nuclear payload.[19]

Russian and Chinese technology have heavily influenced the Iranian missile program, specifically SCUD-B and SCUD-C systems that were acquired in the 1980s and early 1990s. The Shahab-1 and Shahab-2 are believed to be export versions of these Russian missiles. Over the past decade, Iran's focus has progressed to expanding the operational ranges of its missiles, leading to the production of the Shahab-3, an intermediate-range ballistic missile. Likely derived from the North Korean No-Dong 1, Shahab-3 possesses a range of approximately 1,000-1,500 km, allowing it to hit targets in Israel and throughout the Middle East. Iran is estimated to have "dozens" of operational Shahab-3 missiles, as well as variants (Shahab-3A/B, Shahab-4, and BM-25) that are reported to have somewhat longer ranges of between 1,500 and 2,500 km, potentially threatening Turkey and Southern Europe.[20] More pessimistic analyses estimate that Iran ultimately seeks

---

[18] *The Military Balance 2011*, London: International Institute for Strategic Studies, pp. 36–37.

[19] Dennis C. Blair, "Annual Threat Assessment of the U.S. Intelligence Community for the Senate Select Committee on Intelligence," Director of National Intelligence, February 2, 2010, p. 13.

[20] Steven A. Hildreth, "Iran's Ballistic Missile Programs: An Overview," Washington: Congressional Research Service, 2009.

an operational ICBM capability to project power outside of the region.[21] Nonetheless, considered with Iran's ongoing nuclear program, Iran's existing intermediate-range missile capability is a significant challenge for the regional security of the Middle East and, more broadly, the international community.

Iran's short- and intermediate-range conventional ballistic missiles confront the United States and its allies with the threat of retaliatory strikes against key regional targets in the event of a conflict. However, given the relatively limited capabilities of Iran's conventional missile program, particularly the relative inaccuracy of the SCUD-based models, and even the Shahab-3 and its variants, these systems are likely to play two operational roles. First, these missiles may be launched against large U.S. bases—including Ali Al Salem in Kuwait, Al-Udeid in Qatar, Al-Dhafra in the UAE, and perhaps Incirlik in Turkey—in order to disrupt U.S. air operations. [22] Additionally, Iran's missiles may be utilized in a punitive counter-value campaign against population centers in the region, and perhaps oil production infrastructure in Saudi Arabia and the Gulf states, to intimidate opposing regimes and perhaps limit cooperation with U.S. forces.[23] The limited technical capabilities of the Iranian missile systems, particularly their relative inaccuracy and reliance on primitive conventional warheads, are unlikely to provide Iran with a capacity to execute a highly coordinated first-strike against high-value U.S. and allied military targets in the region.[24] While a preventive or preemptive missile strike launched in the midst of an intense diplomatic crisis cannot be ruled out, the inherent technical limitations of these missiles undermine their military effectiveness and would seem to make their employment as anything other than retaliatory weapons improbable.

In considering the capacity of the United States to effectively respond to the current threat of Iranian missiles, it seems clear that

---

[21] National Intelligence Council, 2001.

[22] Davis et al., 2011, p. 34.

[23] Fitzpatrick, 2010, p. 133.

[24] Ibid., pp. 121–25.

the United States possesses significant conventional military capabilities deployed in the Persian Gulf Region and afloat in the Arabian Sea and Indian Ocean to deter or, if necessary, defend against Iranian aggression. Beyond its extensive ongoing deployments in Iraq and Afghanistan, the United States has approximately 50,000 troops and significant materiel in Kuwait. More importantly, the United States has an overwhelming advantage in tactical airpower in the region deployed at the above-mentioned air bases, and these capabilities can quickly be supplemented by U.S. Air Force deployment in Europe and U.S. Navy air assets afloat nearby. Long-range strike programs such as the B-2, B-1, and B-52 bombers further provide the United States with an ability to strike high-value Iranian targets, including their missiles forces, military support infrastructure, and command and control targets in the event of a conflict.[25]

To further mitigate the Iranian missile threat, the United States and its allies in the region have engaged in significant cooperation on missile defenses. Patriot batteries deployed in several Gulf Cooperation Council (GCC) states, including Kuwait and the UAE. Extensive and advanced Patriot and Terminal High Altitude Area Defense (THAAD) in Israel contribute a robust missile defense capability. In addition, the U.S. Navy has deployed *Aegis*-capable cruisers and destroyers to the Mediterranean Sea to bolster land-based missile defense systems deployed in the Gulf Region.[26]

Given the extensive conventional military capabilities that the United States currently deploys in the Gulf region, its capacity to expand upon those capabilities from outside the region, and its current and improving missile defense capabilities, the potential contribution of a new land-based intermediate-range conventional ballistic missile system to deter Iranian provocation seems questionable. U.S. strike aircraft in the region and long-range platforms provide the United States with a capacity to strike targets within Iran, including missile forces and associated targets. In short, the imbalance between U.S. and Iranian conventional military capabilities presents Tehran with the

---

[25] Davis et al., 2011, p. 41.

[26] Ibid., pp. 41–42.

prospect of prohibitively high costs should they engage in provocative behavior, and the availability of missile defenses significantly increases the risks and decreases the potential military benefits of using of those missiles. Under these conditions, the deployment of land-based conventional IRBMs by the United States would seem unnecessary. It is similarly difficult to argue that the United States' deployment of these types of weapons would contribute to dissuading Iran from making a decision to develop nuclear weapons. Precisely because of the overwhelming capabilities the regime currently faces, it seems implausible that the addition of a conventional land-based IRBM would alter the regime's calculations.

The achievement of a nuclear breakthrough by Iran would confront the United States with a potentially acute security challenge. It is beyond the scope of this paper to comprehensively examine the implications of this development. However, with the introduction of an Iranian nuclear capability, including nuclear-capable intermediate-range missiles, some regional security developments may be expected. First, a highly unstable relationship between Iran and Israel likely would develop, given their long-term rivalry. Israel could face significant pressures to launch a disarming first-strike against the Iranian program to preempt an attack or to prevent the acquisition of a larger and more secure second-strike capability. Similarly, Iranian planners could face a consistent pressure to "use or lose" their new capabilities, given the highly uneven nature of the military balance between the two states.[27] Moreover, experts have expressed fears of further proliferation of nuclear weapons programs, based upon planned civilian nuclear energy programs in many states in the region. For example, Saudi Arabia possesses a CSS-2 intermediate range missile that could be fitted with nuclear warheads, perhaps provided by Pakistan.[28] These are certainly troubling developments for the United States, but while Iran's acquisition of nuclear weapons has significant political and security implications for the Middle East and beyond, it is not clear that

---

[27] Lindsay and Takeyh, 2010, p. 39.

[28] Eric Edelman, Andrew Krepinevich, and Evan Braden Montgomery, 2011; Lindsay and Takeyh, 2010, p. 40.

the military challenge facing the United States would be significantly transformed.

In considering whether the United States possesses adequate capabilities to address the Iranian nuclear threat, we can return to the conventional military forces deployed in the region, as well as those capable of rapidly responding to a regional crisis, and the deployment of missile defenses, discussed above. These capabilities will continue to confront Tehran with prohibitively high costs in the event of a conflict, and undermine the confidence that Iranian missiles will achieve their objectives. U.S. forward bases and installations will be at far greater risk of damage or destruction from nuclear-armed, intermediate-range missiles. However, without a significant enhancement of Iranian air defense capabilities, fighter aircraft, or both, the United States would still be expected to achieve air superiority in a conflict and able to strike high-value targets, including Iranian missile forces, even if responding from European bases or U.S. aircraft carriers. More generally, in any consideration of utilizing nuclear weapons, Iranian leaders must assume that these expansive conventional military forces and defensive capabilities are supported by a strategic triad of U.S. ICBMs, as well as SLBMs, and nuclear-capable long-range bombers. These can be visibly deployed to bases in Europe or Diego Garcia and will allow for devastating retaliatory strikes anywhere in Iran.[29]

Moreover, the existence of robust Israeli conventional airpower capabilities, and a formidable intermediate-range missile program, should bolster the deterrent capability U.S. forces provide. It also would confront Tehran with the clear prospect of massive retaliation in the event of a nuclear attack. It is difficult to know exactly what the Israeli missile program entails, but it is believed to have a significant stock of Jericho-2 intermediate-range missiles and approximately 200 operational nuclear warheads that could be delivered by missile or strike aircraft.[30]

Outside the region, the United States also has undertaken a variety of diplomatic and military initiatives to address the poten-

---

[29] Davis et al., 2011, p. 42.

[30] *The Military Balance*, 2011.

tial threat of an Iranian intermediate-range nuclear missile capability. They include the 2009 decision to alter the Bush administration's European missile defense plans to deploy a "Phased Adaptive Approach" based upon U.S. Aegis cruisers and planned radar facilities in Poland and Romania.[31] This supports existing regionally deployed U.S. BMD capabilities and further undermines the potential effectiveness of Iran's intermediate-range missiles and thus their capacity to threaten European targets with nuclear weapons.

As discussed above, the United States' deployment of land-based intermediate-range conventional ballistic missiles seems to offer a capability that seems redundant to existing capabilities. Land-based conventional IRBMs are counterforce weapons, capable of striking high-value targets even under highly contested conditions. Yet precisely because of the existing conventional superiority of the United States, conventional alternatives exist to effectively address these targets. Moreover, if necessary, the United States could rely on central strategic systems, such as SLBMs, ICBMs, or gravity bombs delivered by long-range penetrating bombers.

The only argument that could be made in favor of a deployment of land-based IRBMs to the region would essentially be a *political* one. If an Iranian breakthrough significantly undermined the credibility of the U.S. deterrent guarantee to its regional allies, which ultimately rests on perceptions of political will and commitment, then the action of deploying these weapons could reaffirm America's commitment and dispel other nations' concerns. The missiles themselves would have little added conventional military benefit, but would make a symbolic contribution to reassure allies shaken by the Iranian breakthrough.

At the same time, while having little additional military benefit for the United States, the attributes of a land-based intermediate-range conventional U.S. missile—its visibility, proximity, speed, and high accuracy—would present Iranian planners with a highly threatening counterforce capability that could, in a highly compressed time frame, significantly degrade its military power, threaten its nuclear deterrent, and perhaps its leadership targets. Thus the deployment of

---

[31] Hildreth and Eck, 2009.

U.S. intermediate-range ballistic missile could intensify the pressures on the Iranian regime to use their missiles or risk losing them in the event of a crisis. The potential for such a system to undermine crisis and first-strike stability would significantly limit its—albeit redundant—contribution to enhancing U.S. capabilities to deter an Iranian attack. Finally, obtaining suitable bases for missiles in Egypt, Turkey, Saudi Arabia, or the GCC states would present formidable diplomatic challenges, placing the state in question squarely in the frontline of a potential conflict with a nuclear adversary in a region in which there is relatively strong domestic political opposition to U.S. policies.

Existing U.S. conventional military capabilities, supported by robust and expanding missile defenses, and a credible threat of nuclear retaliation should continue to provide an effective deterrent to Iranian coercion or provocation, and significantly undermine the perceived military effectiveness of its missile programs. Even in the event of Iran acquiring a nuclear weapons capability, the introduction of U.S. conventional, land-based IRBMs would have little impact on addressing this threat. But it likely would intensify the threat that the Iranian regime perceives from the United States and increase the probability of conflict.

The North Korean Missile Threat

North Korea remains one of the more intractable security challenges facing the United States.[32] Given the historical unpredictability of the Kim regime and the limited diplomatic leverage that can be brought to bear on an already-isolated state, the United States and its allies are left with a default policy of containment. Though its closed society presents difficulties in constructing concrete assessments of its capabilities, Pyongyang maintains an active, if limited, nuclear weapons program as well as a significant ballistic missile program initially based on extensive

---

[32] Mark Fitzpatrick, "North Korean Security Challenges: A Net Assessment," Washington: International Institute for Strategic Studies, 2011.

Russian cooperation.[33] The primary role of the nuclear and missile programs is to ensure regime survival and deter any U.S. or South Korean offensive actions, while also providing a capacity to extract concessions from the United States and regional powers.[34] Despite intensive diplomatic efforts during the 1990s characterized by the Agreed Framework, in which the United States effectively offered to aid Pyongyang to develop civilian nuclear power in return for a commitment to forego indigenous plutonium production and uranium enrichment, relations broke down and North Korea withdrew from the Nonproliferation Treaty in January 2003. While North Korea returned to negotiations, engaging in Six-Party talks (with the United States, South Korea, Japan, China, and Russia) from 2003 to 2006, it frustrated its partners by conducting its first nuclear tests in October 2006. During that period, Pyongyang has also conducted several missiles tests of longer-range missile systems with limited success.[35] While the Kim regime sought to portray these tests as satellite launchers, the tests reinforced concerns in Washington about the perceived long-term commitment to develop an ICBM capability that could eventually threaten the United States.

In the past several years, the regime's provocative actions have significantly intensified threat perceptions in the region and further questioned the regime's intentions. In March 2010, the South Korean naval vessel *Cheonan* was sunk near the disputed maritime boundary. After a United Nations–sponsored international investigation, it was determined that a North Korean submarine-fired torpedo sunk the ship. In November 2010, North Korea launched an unprovoked artillery attack on Yeonpyeong Island. The attacks and the subsequent revelation in November 2010 that the North possessed a relatively advanced, operational uranium-enrichment facility, precipitated conservative South Korean politicians' public calls to consider

---

[33] Steven A. Hildreth, "North Korean Ballistic Missile Threat to the United States," Washington: Congressional Research Service, 2009.

[34] Victor D. Cha, "What Do They Really Want?: Obama's North Korea Conundrum," *Washington Quarterly*, Vol. 32, No. 4, 2009.

[35] Narushige Michishita, "Playing the Same Game: North Korea's Coercive Attempt at U.S. Reconciliation," *Washington Quarterly*, Vol. 32, No. 4, 2009.

the reintroduction of U.S. tactical nuclear weapons to deter future attacks. However, the Lee Myung-bak government rejected those calls and reaffirmed its commitment to the 1992 Joint Declaration on the Denuclearization of the Korean Peninsula, even as tensions with the North remained high.[36]

North Korea is believed to possess "hundreds" of SCUD-C and No Dong 1 missiles that are capable of hitting targets in South Korea and Japan, and has seemingly bolstered its regional power projection capability with intermediate-range systems, including the Taepo Dong 1 (~2000 km) and Taepo Dong 2 (~3500-5000 km). The secretive Musudan program also is believed to be an intermediate-range missile system derived from the former Soviet SLBM SS-N-26. Questions have arisen concerning the technical difficulties in suc-cessfully achieving such a derivative program, but it seems clear that Pyongyang has purposely sought to increase its ability to threaten targets outside the Korean Peninsula. In 2009, North Korea tested a large nuclear device and is now estimated to possess between two and six operational weapons.[37] Given the relatively primitive nature of the missiles that North Korea has deployed, particularly in terms of accu-racy, it seems likely that they would be utilized as the preferred delivery vehicles for the limited stock of nuclear warheads. Questions remain about the ability of North Korean engineers to develop an effective warhead design for use with its missile forces, but even conservative estimates would seem to indicate that such a capability would be attainable given the time and resources that have been devoted to the project over the past decades. In addition, North Korea is believed to possess between approximately 2,500-3,500 tons of chemical weapons and perhaps a biological weapons program.[38]

The North Korean missile program thus presents the United States with a significant multi-dimensional threat. While the large

---

[36] Kim So-hyun, "Calls Mounting for Return of U.S. Tactical Nukes," *Korea Herald*, March 1, 2011.

[37] Mary Beth Nitkin, "North Korea's Nuclear Weapons: Technical Issues," Washington: Congressional Research Service, 2011.

[38] *The Military Balance,* 2011.

North Korean conventional military has reportedly deteriorated over time, Pyongyang's short- and intermediate-range missiles may play a large role in a future conflict on the peninsula. Shorter-range conventionally- or perhaps chemically-armed missiles and artillery may be expected to target ROK and U.S. forces within reach of the demilitarized zone. Intermediate-range missiles equipped with conventional, nuclear, and perhaps chemical warheads could be aimed at more distant targets, such as U.S. bases in the region or perhaps population centers in Japan, to compel Tokyo to refrain from involvement in a conflict and/or degrade the capacity of the United States to effectively support and reinforce its forces in South Korea.

The United States continues to maintain a robust conventional military presence in South Korea, including more than 25,000 troops, and in East Asia. Moreover, despite the size of the North Korean military, the forces of the Republic of Korea are generally viewed as qualitatively superior to those of the North, though any conflict would be devastating to the South, precisely because of the geography of the Korean peninsula. The United States also has worked closely with Japan to effectively respond to a potential North Korean contingency.

The United States devotes significant missile defense capabilities to the region, most notably the presence of *Aegis*-equipped U.S. naval vessels, with 16 of the Navy's 21 ships deployed in the Pacific.[39] Japan's Maritime Self Defense Force (MSDF) currently deploys four Kongo class *Aegis*-equipped Guided Missile Destroyers (DDG) with SM-3 interceptor missiles, as well as 16 Patriot (PAC-3) missile batteries, and is engaged in jointly developing the SM-3 Block IIA interceptor with the United States.[40] Further planned cooperative development and integration of missile defense capabilities with Japan and South Korea will enhance the capabilities to defend against a potential North Korean intermediate-range missile attack.

---

[39] Ronald O'Rourke, "Navy Aegis Ballistic Missile Defense (BMD) Program: Background and Issues for Congress," Washington: Congressional Research Service, 2010, p. 5.

[40] Bruce Klinger, "Backgrounder No. 2506: The Case for Comprehensive Missile Defense in Asia," Heritage Foundation, January 7, 2011.

U.S. strategic nuclear forces remain the ultimate deterrent against a North Korean use of nuclear or perhaps chemical weapons. Such forces support both the conventional deterrent capabilities deployed in South Korea and in the western Pacific, and the existing and expanding missile defense capabilities in the region. Nuclear or chemical attacks against U.S. forces in the region (or perhaps the U.S. homeland in the future), Japan, or South Korea would ostensibly be met with a retaliatory nuclear strike by the United States. The United States may possess conventional forces capable of achieving the requisite level of destruction to remove the regime, but no leader could assume that a nuclear strike on the United States or its allies would not precipitate a devastating "in kind" response. As discussions in Seoul reflect concerning the reintroduction of tactical nuclear weapons, South Korean confidence in the U.S. extended deterrent commitment is not in question, despite the provocations of the North.

Given these robust conventional capabilities, what contribution would a land-based, conventional IRBM make to U.S. forces? First, a conventional intermediate-range ballistic missile would possess a greater range than necessary for responding to most North Korean targets, if deployed in the South, even if outside of the distance of most short-range North Korean missiles. In fact, any such missile with a capability of greater than 1,500 km presents a threat to China more so than to North Korea. Second, the signal created by the deployment of a highly accurate, conventional IRBM could be seen as provocative. Such a system would seemingly be dedicated to high-value targets, including North Korean regime leadership installations, command and control, and perhaps the nuclear and missile programs and supporting installations. Given the importance of these capabilities to the perceived security of the regime, not to mention the direct threat posed to the regime leaders' physical security, these missiles could significantly increase the threat perceived by the regime, leading to a destabilization of relations and potentially a crisis. While diplomatic initiatives have been suspended in response to the most recent provocations, the participation of other regional states in the management of the North Korean nuclear program is likely to resume.[41]

Finally, basing issues likely are to prove difficult to address. Deployment of such missiles on Japan would, perhaps, more clearly address the North Korean threat, allowing for a wider package of targets and better use of the range and accuracy of the missiles, But it seems highly unlikely that Japan would agree to the basing of such an offensive system because of the likely regional diplomatic implications.

Given the nature of the North Korean regime, it is difficult to assess the level of forces required to effectively deter aggression, as the recent provocations illustrate. Nonetheless, the current deployment of U.S. military capabilities in South Korea, together with ROK forces and additional capabilities deployed in the region, seems sufficient to deter—or, if necessary, defend against—an unprovoked attack by the North. Moreover, the expansion of U.S. and allied missile defense capabilities, and the underlying nuclear guarantee of the United States, further reassures Japan that North Korean provocation will be effectively addressed.

India and Pakistan: Confidence Building and De-escalation

The missile programs of India and Pakistan are reflective of their intense long-term historical rivalry. The two nations have fought four wars since partition after gaining independence from Great Britain in 1949, with the most recent coming in the 1999 Kargil War. The majority-Muslim Indian state of Kashmir continues to serve as a source of conflict, with Pakistan supporting various separatist insurgent and terrorist groups to attack Indian authorities in Kashmir. The investment in short- and intermediate-range missiles is a logical development after the 1998 nuclear tests by both states. India has a long-running and extensive missile development program, stretching back to its successful pro-

---

[41] Mary Beth Sheridan, "U.S. To Send Envoy to North Korea to Consider Food Aid," *Washington Post*, May 20, 2011.

duction of a satellite launch vehicle (SLV) in 1980. With significant technical support from countries such as the United Kingdom, France, the United States, and the Soviet Union, India has built a relatively robust indigenous ballistic missile program.[42] Pakistan, conversely, has been forced to depend in large part on support from China. Both states engaged in the development of short-range conventional tactical missiles prior to achieving nuclear status, and several of their initial nuclear delivery vehicles were predominantly short-range systems. However, more recently, as the nuclear aspect of the rivalry has taken precedence, the desire for greater ranges has led to a focus on intermediate-range systems. Given their geographic proximity, short- and medium-range missile systems suffice to deliver potential nuclear strikes, thus contributing to increasingly formidable deterrent forces.[43] The nature of the competition, and thus the construction of respective missile programs, is not entirely symmetrical, as Pakistan confronts a major quantitative conventional disadvantage and a problem of strategic depth due to its geography. Nuclear weapons have thus taken on a more central role in Pakistan's military doctrine, and recent reports indicate that Pakistan's production of fissile material has outpaced India's.[44] Moreover, Pakistan's use of proxies such as the terrorist group Lashkar-e-Taiba, which carried out the attacks on Mumbai in November 2009, has created an unstable situation that threatens to destabilize the tenuous relationship between the two states. In the face of another Mumbai-like attack, India's leaders would confront strong pressures to retaliate, most likely with a strong show of conventional military force. But even a limited punitive operation—for example, targeting terrorist training camps in Pakistan—may be confused with a larger conventional offense, leading Pakistani leaders to utilize nuclear weapons to de-esca-

---

[42] Gormley, 2008, pp. 35–36.

[43] John E. Peters, James Dickens, Derek Eaton, C. Christine Fair, Nina Hachigan, Theodore W. Karasik, Rollie Lal, Rachel M. Swanger, Gregory F. Treverton, and Charles Wolf Jr., *War and Escalation in South Asia,* Santa Monica, Calif.: RAND Corporation, MG-367-1-AF, 2006.

[44] Dinshaw Mistry, "Tempering Optimism About Nuclear Deterrence in South Asia," *Security Studies, Vol.* 18, 2009.

late the crisis. Considering the conventional military asymmetries, the challenge of the region's geography, and the activity of non-state actors, the nuclear balance on the Subcontinent remains tenuous.[45]

India's missile development has proceeded in concert with a major conventional military modernization program to provide more flexible and credible deterrent options for Indian leaders to respond to Pakistani provocations without relying on nuclear forces.[46] Nonetheless, any Indian conventional response conceivably could spur the Pakistani military to respond with nuclear weapons early on in a conflict, and the potential for rapid and potentially uncontrolled escalation is a persistent danger. Moving beyond the challenge of Pakistan, India's development of intermediate-range missile forces seem more directed toward the expansion of China's military capabilities.[47] Given unresolved border conflicts with China, as well as Beijing's continued support for Pakistan's nuclear programs, India views China with mistrust.

While neither missile program poses a direct threat to the United States, a conflict between India and Pakistan and the potential for a nuclear exchange would have significant implications for U.S. interests and the broader international community. Avoiding a nuclear exchange on the Subcontinent is the overriding U.S. interest. Moreover, with U.S. troops deployed to Afghanistan, it is critical to maintain relations with both states to effectively support the mission there. The potential deployment of U.S. INF missiles seems inappropriate to the discussion of the challenge of India and Pakistani missile programs. However, these programs do have an impact on China and Russia's perceptions of missile threats. Any attempts to address the challenge through trilateral cooperative means will likely have to address those perceptions as well.

---

[45] Peters et al., 2006, pp. 39–41.

[46] Walter C. Ludwig, "A Cold Start for Hot Wars? The Indian Army's New Limited War Doctrine," *International Security,* Vol. 32, No. 3, 2007/08.

[47] David M. Malone and Rohan Mukherjee, "India and China: Conflict and Cooperation," *Survival,* Vol. 52, No. 1, 2010.

Conclusion

The expanding land-based intermediate-range missile programs of Iran and North Korea confront the United States with difficult security challenges in key regions. However, as the analysis in this chapter reflects, the United States does not require an enhancement in conventional military capabilities offered by a new generation of land-based conventional IRBMs to effectively address these threats. Working closely with regional allies and global partners to enhance nonproliferation efforts, deter provocative behavior, and reassure states under threat all would seem to provide more effective means for addressing the threats of North Korea and Iran. Meanwhile, military options seem inappropriate to the management of the Indian and Pakistani programs. In the cases of Iran and North Korea, the United States possesses key attributes of maintaining deterrence in a regional context.[48] With nuclear superiority, increasing active and passive defenses as well as conventional counterforce capabilities to deny the expected benefits of missile strikes, and the requisite intelligence and surveillance capabilities to detect launches and hold critical targets at risk, the United States seems capable of effectively addressing these regional threats. The additional capabilities provided by regional allies such as South Korea and Japan, and Israel and the GCC states further contribute to the capacity to deter North Korean and Iranian aggression, respectively. Iran's achievement of a breakout nuclear capability does represent a significant threat to regional security, particularly considering the pressures to preempt that likely would emerge between Israel and Iran. But under such circumstances, it would seem even more important for the United States to reassure allies and maintain or enhance its capabilities to deter Iran in ways that do not further destabilize the security environment. The United States' deployment of conventional intermediate-range missiles would seem to be especially threatening to the regime in Tehran, and likely would contribute to an intensification of pressures to preempt and contribute to further instability without

---

[48] Ochmanek and Schwartz, 2008.

providing any clear military benefits above and beyond the already formidable U.S. conventional military capabilities in the region.

CHAPTER FOUR

The Challenge of China's Military Modernization

The People's Republic of China's (PRC) extensive military modernization program has already had significant implications for U.S. interests in the Western Pacific. While China has invested in the improvement and expansion of many aspects of its military forces, the development of its conventional ballistic and cruise missile programs confronts the United States with a particularly difficult challenge.[1] Not only has Beijing acquired and deployed ballistic short-range missiles in such quantities as to threaten Taiwan with a potentially disarming strike, but, increasingly, U.S. forward bases, tactical airpower, and naval assets may be at risk as conventional IRBMs and LACMs are deployed in greater numbers. Over time, the balance of forces seems to be shifting against the United States and Taiwan. Precisely because of the nature of the threat, the question arises as to whether the deployment of a land-based intermediate-range conventional ballistic missile system is necessary to enhance U.S. conventional capabilities to effectively deter—or, if necessary, defend against—a Chinese attack on Taiwan. What other alternatives should U.S. policymakers consider? This chapter will analyze the potential utility of new conventional intermediate-range ballistic missiles, as well as other programs, in the context of the growing Chinese missile threat and consider the implications for U.S. security going forward.

---

[1] For the purposes of this discussion, the primary threat of China's short- and intermediate-range missiles is conventional in nature. However, because these systems are reportedly dual use—particularly the CSS-5 IRBM and DH-10 LACM—there is a latent nuclear threat that will be discussed later in the chapter.

First, the nature of the threat confronting the United States will be examined. The second section provides a very basic cost assessment of a new intermediate-range conventional missile system, a "Pershing-III," after examining existing and potential future alternative programs. The third section will assess the case for U.S. land-based, intermediate-range conventional missiles and evaluate their potential contribution to effectively addressing the threat of China's missile deployments. The fourth and final section examines some potential political-military implications that can be expected to arise were the United States to deploy land-based, intermediate-range missiles.

Assessing the Chinese Missile Threat

Nowhere has the vertical proliferation of missile systems been more evident than in the PRC. Pursuing a major military modernization program that started the 1990s, the development of robust short- and medium-range missile capabilities has emerged as a focus of China's efforts. Both the quantity of Chinese short- and medium-range ballistic and cruise missile systems, and the increasing quality of those systems (particularly improvements in accuracy), have shifted the military balance in the Taiwan Straits and increasingly threaten U.S. forces and allies. The modernization and expansion of China's missile force has been extensive, with more than 1,000 shorter-range ballistic missiles (CSS-6 and CSS-7) deployed across from Taiwan.[2] More recently, since 2005, increasing numbers of CSS-5 intermediate-range ballistic missiles with a range of approximately 1,500 km as well as DH-10 ground-based land attack cruise missiles—which are estimated to possess a range of approximately 2,100 km—have significantly expanded the inventory of INF missile forces.[3] The PRC is estimated to have produced approximately 50 to 100 of these intermediate-range cruise mis-

---

[2]   The CSS-6, with a range of approximately 600 km, would fall under the constraints of the INF Treaty, were China to become a member.

[3]   Office of the Secretary of Defense, *Annual Report to Congress: Military Power of the People's Republic of China*, 2010.

Figure 4.1
China's Missile Development Programs in Context

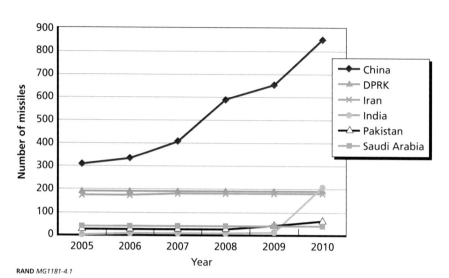

RAND *MG1181-4.1*

NOTE: Estimates of intermediate-range missile programs from International Institute for Strategic Studies, *Military Balance*, 2005-2010 (London); China intermediate-range ballistic and cruise missile estimates from Office of the Secretary of Defense, *Report on the Military Power of the People's Republic of China 2005-2010* (Washington, DC).

siles per year over the past three years. The CSS-5 is also believed to be the basis of a "carrier-killer" anti-ship ballistic missile variant that has received a significant amount of interest because of the potential threat to U.S. naval assets in the region.[4]

The nature of the threat created by China's expanding missile force has grown over time.[5] First, these capabilities seemingly provide Beijing with a robust capacity to coerce Taiwan, ostensibly to deter

---

[4]   Erickson and Yang, 2009.

[5]   James C. Mulvenon Murray Scot Tanner, Michael S. Chase, David Frelinger, David C. Gompert, Martin C. Libiki, and Kevin L. Pollpeter, *Chinese Responses to U.S. Military Transformation and Implications for the Department of Defense,* Santa Monica, Calif.: RAND Corporation, MG-340-OSD, 2006; David A. Shlapak, David T. Orletsky, and Barry Wilson, *Dire Strait?: Military Aspects of the China-Taiwan Confrontation and Options for U.S. Policy* Santa Monica, Calif.: RAND Corporation, MR-1217-SRF, 2000.

Taiwanese leaders from unilaterally declaring independence or compelling a reversal of a declaration should deterrence fail. China's quantity of conventional short- and medium-range conventional missiles has shifted the cross-Straits' military balance. The missile forces could be utilized to saturate Taiwan's air defense, destroy much of Taiwan's air force on the ground, and seize air superiority, as a recent RAND analysis explains:[6]

> As China's ability to deliver accurate fire across the straits grows, *it is becoming increasingly difficult and soon may be impossible for the United States and Taiwan to protect the island's military and civilian infrastructures from serious damage.*[7]

Second, as the size and reach of the missile force grows—particularly stocks of CSS-5 ballistic missiles and DH-10 cruise missiles—U.S. forces that can be expected to support Taiwan's defense increasingly are under risk. Specifically, the U.S. airbase at Kadena on Okinawa, Kunsan Air Base in South Korea, and U.S. naval forces in the region may be targets of preventive strikes to degrade the capabilities of the United States to intervene on Taiwan's behalf in the event of a crisis. With U.S. forward bases knocked offline, the United States would likely be left to launch operations from Andersen Air Force base on Guam and from U.S. Navy assets in the region, which now must do so outside a certain perimeter to operate safely. Experts on Chinese military affairs argue that China possesses a growing Anti-Access/Area-Denial (AA/AD) capability, which experts define as follows:[8]

> ...[W]e considered an anti-access measure to be any action by an opponent that has the effect of slowing the deployment of friendly forces into a theater, preventing them from operating from certain locations within the theater, or causing them to operate from

---

[6] Shlapak et al., 2009, pp. 128–129.

[7] Ibid., p. 126. Italics in original.

[8] Andrew Krepinevich, Barry Watts, and Robert Work, *Meeting the Anti-Access and Area Denial Challenge,* Washington: Center for Strategic and Budgetary Assessments, 2003.

distances farther from the locus of conflict than they would normally prefer.[9]

While a strategy of AA/AD is not explicitly used in Chinese military writings, several concepts combine to imply that Chinese military strategists are thinking along these lines. "Seizing the initiative" and "active defense," where Chinese forces could be utilized in preventive, offensive operations to achieve ostensibly defensive objectives, are precisely the kinds of concepts that would underlie a broader AA/AD strategy in the event of a conflict. Thus the combination of Chinese capabilities and emerging doctrine seem focused on keeping the United States beyond the so-called "First island chain," which would significantly complicate efforts to relieve and reinforce Taiwan in the event of a conflict. At this point, air superiority over Taiwan would be contested, but over time it may become increasingly difficult to achieve.[10] It is important to note that it is not clear China would attack U.S. forward bases at the outset of a conflict. However, given the continuing buildup of missiles, these bases are increasingly at risk. Considering China's expansion of its missile capabilities and other forces, including fighter and strike aircraft and information and space warfare capabilities, the defense of Taiwan confronts the United States with a challenge that is seemingly getting more difficult.[11]

Finally, a longer-term potential threat has received less analytical focus than the potentially disarming strike scenario against Taiwan and the potentially larger AA/AD campaign against the United States: the Chinese decision to equip some significant portion of its intermediate-range missiles, particularly the CSS-5 (and perhaps the DH-10 as well), with nuclear warheads. Because of the opaque nature of China's military modernization, it is difficult to estimate how many of the currently deployed CSS-5 missiles have been equipped with

---

[9]   Roger Cliff, Mark Burles, Michael S. Chase, Derek Eaton, and Kevin L. Pollpeter, *Entering the Dragon's Lair: Chinese Antiaccess Strategies and Their Implications for the United States* Santa Monica, Calif.: RAND Corporation, MG-524-AF, 2007.

[10]   Shlapak et al., 2009, p. 135.

[11]   Ibid.

Figure 4.2
Map

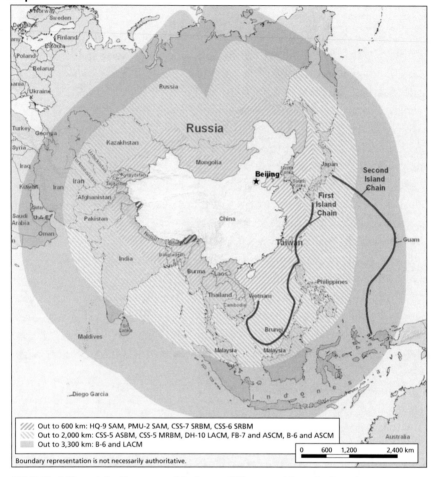

SOURCE: Office of the Secretary of Defense, *Military and Security Developments Involving the People's Republic of China*, 2010, p. 32.
RAND MG1181-4.2

nuclear warheads, but the dual-capable missile has been a program that has expanded significantly over the past five years. One recent estimate places the number of CSS-5 launchers devoted to nuclear missions at 80, while 36 launchers are employed for conventional missions.[12] Recent U.S. Senate deliberations over the ratification of the "New START" Treaty in Washington were marked by concerns that China could "sprint up" to U.S. levels in strategic forces if further reductions were carried out.[13] However, the equipping of existing intermediate-range missiles with nuclear warheads would seem to be a feasible alternative means to achieve a formidable nuclear force capable of bolstering China's influence in the region, rather than focusing on a new generation of ICBMs that directly targets the United States. The "sprint up" scenario could thus manifest as a regional rather than global strategy. Much of the existing literature on Chinese nuclear doctrine and strategy would seem to attach a low probability to such a policy, but the sheer number of delivery vehicles that China continues to develop and deploy creates a latent capability that could be used to coerce its regional neighbors in the future.[14] Given U.S. interests in the region and its alliances with Japan and the Republic of Korea (ROK), this is a significant potential threat.

In summary, China's missile modernization confronts the United States with an acute challenge precisely because it threatens what have typically been considered crucial assets of traditional U.S. power projection. Holding forward bases and tactical aircraft in the region at risk undermines the U.S. capacity to promptly and effectively respond to crises. Moreover, with forward bases knocked offline and tactical airpower assets significantly degraded, the burden of responding to a crisis would fall more heavily on U.S. naval assets. However, with increases in Chinese airpower and the emerging threat of anti-ship ballistic missiles, the U.S. Navy's ability to carry out operations in the vicinity of the Taiwan Straits may also be increasingly difficult. Finally, the expansion of ballistic and cruise missiles seriously undermine the potential contri-

---

[12] *The Military Balance,* 2011.

[13] Peter Brookes, "New START Treaty's China Challenge," *New York Post,* September 20, 2010.

[14] M. Taylor Fravel and Evan S. Medeiros, "China's Search for Assured Retaliation: The Evolution of Chinese Nuclear Strategy and Force Structure," *International Security,* Vol. 35, No. 2, 2010; Jeffrey Lewis, *The Minumum Means of Reprisal: China's Search for Security in the Nuclear Age,* Cambridge: The MIT Press, 2007.

butions of U.S. theater ballistic missile defenses (TBMD).[15] As recent analyses have concluded, given the tradeoff between anti-missile interceptors and China's short- and medium-range ballistic missile force, the prospects of large-scale defenses are prohibitively costly. While BMD may alter the adversary's calculations at the margins, beyond certain quantities, active defense are simply not going to be capable of effectively fulfilling missions like defending unsheltered aircraft on runways. Even if missile defenses are presumed to be relatively effective, there are considerations that limit their expected utility in conflict scenarios. First, missile defenses, radar installations, and interceptors may themselves be the targets of suppression strikes early in a conflict, potentially with cruise missiles, degrading deployed U.S. capabilities in the region. Second, U.S. theater missile defense capabilities are finite and can thus be overwhelmed by the sheer number of Chinese missiles.[16] This quantitative advantage in intermediate-range missiles would seem to limit the marginal utility of investments in active U.S. defenses moving forward.

Considering a "Pershing III" vs. Potential Alternative Programs

The United States has two broad means of decreasing the potential benefits of a Chinese conventional first strike. Washington can raise the potential costs, or decrease the potential benefits and increase the expected risk associated with a successful operation (or some combination of the two). The first approach would entail the deployment of forces that enhance the U.S. deterrent in the region, while the latter would focus on enhancing the capacity of U.S. forces to deny China from achieving their military objectives. A new land-based, intermediate-range missile would be a potential candidate to enhance the conventional capabilities of the United States and thus enhance its ability

---

[15] Marshall Hoyler, "China's 'Antiaccess' Ballistic Missiles and U.S. Active Defenses," *Naval War College Review*, Vol. 63, No. 4, 2010.

[16] Shlapak et al., 2009, pp. 125–26.

to deter a Chinese attack. The second approach, improving the ability of U.S. forces to deny the expected benefits of a Chinese attack by mitigating the likely effects or increasing the risk of failure, would typically involve the enhancement of active and passive defense. However, as discussed above, the quantitative expansion of China's missile forces seems to present real constraints for the potential contribution of defenses, and the costs of such programs may prove prohibitive. Ultimately, then, some mix of deterrence and denial may be optimal from both an operational and cost-effectiveness calculation. Moreover, these programmatic alternatives can be considered in short-, medium-, and longer-term investments as well as ongoing efforts to improve U.S. capabilities vis-à-vis China's military modernization (see Table 4.1 below).

Existing Options for Bolstering U.S. Capabilities in the Short Term
Despite the constraints of the INF Treaty, the United States remains capable of deploying robust conventional capabilities in the East Asian region to bolster its current force posture if decisionmakers deem such an improvement necessary. In considering current assets available to U.S. planners to effectively respond to a growing imbalance in conventional forces in the region, the Ohio-class SSGN-726 or "Tactical Trident" may be expected to make a significant contribution.[17] First, the guided (cruise) missile submarine (SSGN) can carry 154 Tomahawk Land Attack Missiles (TLAM) or the equivalent of a battle group's full capacity of cruise missiles, which can be launched at rapid rates. Moreover, given its ability to operate in otherwise denied areas thanks to its endurance and stealth, the SSGN provides a robust capability to maintain U.S. firepower in the event of a Chinese attack. The U.S. Navy currently deploys four of the Ohio-Class SSGN-726s, which were converted from nuclear-armed SSBNs in the 1990s for approximately $400 million each. The USS Ohio and USS Michigan are deployed in the Pacific, while the USS Florida and USS Georgia are deployed in the Atlantic. In the event of a crisis, the movement of these four submarines to the western Pacific would send a

---

[17] "Ohio-Class SSGN-726 Tactical Trident," *GlobalSecurity.Org*, 2011.

Table 4.1
Assessing a New Intermediate-Range Ballistic Missile and Potential Alternatives

	Current, Short-term	Medium-term	Long-term
Deterrent Capabilities	• SSGNs with TLAM • Maintain/Enhance stocks of TLAM, Tactical TLAM, and PGMs • B-2 (limited) • B-1 with JSAM	• Arsenal ship • Arsenal plane (modified P-8) • JSAM-ER • Tactical TLAM-X	• Next-generation LRS • Penetrating/Standoff • Ship-launched ballistic missile • SSGN-X • Prompt Global Strike • Conventional SLBM
Defense/Denial Capabilities	• Deploy Aegis Ships • Pac-2, Pac-3 BMDs • Runway recovery packages	• Enhance AD, TBMD, TCMD • Harden air bases and infrastructure	• Diversify basing options • Enhance allied capabilities
C4ISR Capabilities (Improve throughout)	• Harden/reduce existing vulnerabilities in systems • Early warning capabilities	• Detect, identify, attack mobile, time-sensitive targets	• EMP mitigation • ASAT countermeasures • Enhance offensive info/e-warfare capabilities

strong signal of U.S. resolve and significantly bolster U.S. capabilities in the region. In June 2010, this type of signal was sent when three of the four SSGNs arrived in strategically important ports: the USS Michigan in Pusan, South Korea, the USS Ohio in Subic Bay, Philippines, and the USS Florida in Diego Garcia.[18] If the United States maintains investments in high levels of precision-guided munitions, including the so-called "Tactical Tomahawk," and deployed replacement munitions in the theater—at Guam, for example—the SSGN fleet could contribute to significant enhancement of U.S. firepower capabilities in the region for a sustained period. Maintaining this capability, and perhaps expanding it through the conversion of other submarines or committing a certain number of new submarines to the "Tactical Trident" mission, would provide a consistent, survivable, and flexible asset to deter or effectively defend against a potential conflict in the Western Pacific.

In the short term, investments can be made to sustain and enhance the standoff capability of the B-1 and B-52 forces with improvements of air-launched cruise missiles that can be fired from outside the range of Chinese anti-air and fighter capabilities. While an updated variant of the Joint Air-to-Surface Standoff Missile (JASSM) has been procured to achieve longer-ranges, it is unclear that with a maximum range of 500 nautical miles (805 km), the JASSM-ER (Extended Range) is sufficient for a Taiwan crisis scenario. A B-1 can carry 21 of these missiles, but would currently have to approach contested airspace to deliver them to targets. Similarly, sea-launched cruise missiles, such as the Tactical Tomahawk, carried by surface vessels and from Ohio-class SSGNs, provide a capability to threaten Chinese targets and can be procured in larger numbers if policymakers deem necessary.

Alternative Options for Enhancing U.S. Capabilities in the Medium Term

Other programs could also enhance U.S. deterrence capabilities in the region in the medium term. One candidate would be the resur-

---

[18] Mark Thompson, "U.S. Missiles Deployed near China Send a Message," *Time*, July 8, 2010.

rection of the "Arsenal Ship" concept, which was considered in the mid-1990s but ultimately rejected.[19] The ship was presented as a relatively cost-effective means (ostensibly $520 million in 1996 dollars) of providing significant firepower capabilities to a theater commander.[20] With plans for 512 Vertical Launch System (VLS) cells, four to six of these vessels would have greatly enhanced the U.S. conventional firepower capability in the region and would have had the added benefit of presenting Chinese planners with a number of a additional targets to address, creating significant complications.[21] Some experts also have considered a surface vessel, like the arsenal ship, that could carry a sea-launched intermediate-range ballistic missile.[22] This would represent a major expansion of capabilities, though it may present some problems vis-à-vis the spirit, if not letter, of the INF Treaty. Similarly, there has been a discussion of an "arsenal airplane" that would carry a large number of cruise missiles and greatly enhance the standoff capability of U.S. airpower. The Boeing P-8A Poseidon, currently under development by the U.S. Navy as a Multi-Mission Aircraft (MMA) for Anti-Submarine Warfare (ASW) and Anti-Surface Warfare (ASUW) as well as Intelligence Surveillance and Reconnaissance (ISR), is based on a Boeing 737 jet frame.[23] Equipping a similar civilian-based jet with advanced, long-range cruise missiles would likely be more expensive than the Poseidon's $280 million unit cost, but a sufficiently sized fleet of these aircraft could address any perceived gap in capabilities.[24] With the exception of the ballistic-missile vessel, these programs would seem

---

[19] Robert S. Leonard, Jeffrey Drezner, and Geoffrey Sommer, *The Arsenal Ship Acquisition Process Experience: Contrasting and Common Impressions from the Contractor Teams and Joint Program Office,* Santa Monica, Calif.: RAND Corporation, MR-1030-DARPA, 1999.

[20] "Arsenal Ship," Federation of American Scientists, no date.

[21] Scott C. Truver, "Floating Arsenal to Be 21st Century Battleship," *International Defense Review,* Vol. 29, No. 7, 1996.

[22] Jan Van Tol, Mark Gunzinger, Andrew Krepinevich, and Jim Thomas, *Airsea Battle: A Point of Departure Operational Concept,* Washington: Center for Strategic and Budgetary Assessments, 2010, pp. 83–84.

[23] Flynn, 2008.

[24] U.S. Department of Defense, *Selected Acquistion Report (SAR).* November 12, 2010.

to be relatively cost-effective solutions to the Chinese missile modernization program without the program costs of land-based missiles and without necessitating a withdrawal from the INF Treaty.

Alternative Options for Enhancing U.S. Capabilities in the Long Term
Concerns about the ability of U.S. tactical aircraft to respond from forward bases because of the threat of Chinese missiles is seemingly made more acute by the perception of a decrease in U.S. long-range strike capabilities. The small size of the B-2 force, the limited capabilities of the B-1 bomber, and the age of the B-52 force have created such a perception.[25] With Chinese investments in modern air defense systems, early warning, and command and control capabilities, the ability of older, non-stealthy, long-range platforms such as the B-52 and B-1 to carry out missions over mainland China is no longer tenable. The perceived need for follow-on to the B-2 has been argued elsewhere, and given the importance of maintaining a long-range strike capability, decisions on long-term investments will have significant implications for U.S. power projection beyond this scenario.[26] The size and costs of such a program can vary significantly, depending on the analysis, but 100 to 175 aircraft for approximately $40 to $50 billion provides some sense of the magnitude.[27] Moreover, a significant emerging tradeoff seems to involve whether to defer the program to take advantage of technologies that will be available in 2020, or to attempt to build a less expensive platform based on existing, off-the-shelf technologies that could significantly influence the ultimate price of the program.[28] The decision to invest in a next-generation long-range bomber will obviously take into account a variety of threats as well as cost issues,

---

[25] Jeremiah J. Gertler, *Air Force Next-Generation Bomber: Background and Issues for Congress,* Washington: Congressional Research Service, 2009.

[26] Robert Haffa and Michael Isherwood, *The 2018 Bomber: The Case for Accelerating the Next Generation Long-Range Strike System,* Washington: Northrop Grumman, 2008.

[27] Mark Gunzinger, *Sustaining America's Advantage in Long-Range Strike,* Washington: Center for Strategic and Budgetary Assessments, 2010, pp. 60–62; Dave Majumdar, "U.S. Air Force May Buy 175 Bombers," *Defense News,* January 24, 2011.

[28] Gunzinger, 2010, pp. 63–65.

and a new intermediate-range ballistic missile would be much smaller in scope and thus a fraction of the overall costs. However, given the constrained fiscal environment facing the Department of Defense, the question arises as to where those resources are best spent.

Enhancing Denial Capabilities

Improving the U.S. ability to deny Chinese objectives would focus on three main areas: the improvement of active defense, the improvement of passive defense, and the enhancement of surveillance and reconnaissance capabilities to maintain early warning and avoid suffering a disarming first-strike. The United States has made significant progress in the development of theater missile defense. The U.S. Navy's Aegis system has proven effective in addressing limited missile attacks under test conditions.[29] However, missile defenses face the fundamental problem of numbers, and given the finite number of Aegis cruisers and destroyers and their commitment to other regions, the Chinese missile buildup presents real problems for an active defense strategy. Even taking into consideration the cooperative Japanese missile defense capability, it is highly unlikely that the United States will ever be able to bring enough missile defense to the region to be decisive in a conflict. At some point, they are likely to be overwhelmed. Nonetheless, they contribute to U.S. posture by complicating China's cost-benefit and risk assessments. There are currently few available defenses against advanced cruise missiles. This problem has received greater attention recently but, like ballistic missile defense, it continues to present planners with relatively unfavorable cost tradeoffs.[30]

Passive defense further undermines China's planning by allowing U.S. bases to absorb and recover from a strike.[31] In the short term, investing in capabilities to strengthen—and, if necessary, repair—runways would significantly mitigate the effects of a missile attack. Similarly, hardening of existing bases and building additional shel-

---

[29] Ronald O'Rourke, *Navy Aegis Ballistic Missile Defense (BMD) Program: Background and Issues for Congress,* Washington: Congressional Research Service, 2010.

[30] Malone and Mukherjee, 2010.

[31] Cliff et al., 2007, pp. 95–97.

ters and underground fuel tanks may be costly, but such moves could potentially improve the ability to withstand an attack and maintain operational tempo. Over the longer term, the potential diversification of U.S. forward bases in the Western Pacific also may be beneficial, but will require extensive diplomatic and political activity as well as economic resources.

Another alternative is the "hardening" and expansion of U.S. command, control, communications, computers, intelligence, surveillance, and reconnaisance (C4ISR) capabilities in the region to achieve early warning and to maintain a robust capacity for situational awareness. This would likely necessitate investment in various cyber and space capabilities as well, to allow the United States to withstand a "blinding" or "dazzling" attack by China that may precede or accompany a missile assault on U.S. forces. Such assets also may allow the United States to degrade or hinder the ability of the PLA to coordinate and execute its attack, mitigate the damage of an attack, and improve the U.S. capacity to respond.[32]

What should be clear from this analysis is that the value of both active and passive defenses is likely to erode over time with a further expansion of Chinese missile forces. At best, U.S. decisions can offset China's advantages, but they are unlikely to overcome them in a cost-effective way. In recognizing the fundamentally uneven nature of this competition, planners and decision-makers may be left to focus on alternatives that enhance U.S. conventional capabilities to deter a Chinese attack. The key question is whether the United States requires a new land-based, intermediate-range conventional ballistic missile to achieve those capabilities.

A Pershing III Land-Based Conventional IRBM for the Pacific?

The program costs associated with the development of a new, highly capable intermediate-range missile should be considered. The Pershing II program, which ultimately produced 234 missiles, would cost

---

[32] Van Tol et al., 2010.

approximately $4.3 billion in current (2011) dollars.[33] To provide a rough, basic estimate of quantities of Pershing IIIs the United States may wish to deploy in the Pacific, an initial deployment of approximately 600 missiles would seem to provide the quantity required to target a number of China's key air bases, which likely would be used in the event of a conflict with Taiwan.[34] Thus, in very rough terms, the initial program cost could be estimated to be approximately $12 billion. However, several factors may contribute to a more costly system. First, the attributes of a Pershing III would almost certainly require a range of at least 3,500 km—almost twice the Pershing II (1,800 km)—to effectively threaten the Guangzhou and Nanjing military districts across from Taiwan, and perhaps ranges in excess of 4,000 km to strike critical targets in Central China from an initial basing on Guam. As will be discussed later in this chapter and the next chapter, deployment of a new U.S. conventional, land-based IRBM may be a diplomatic challenge and could be politically problematic for regional allies. Diverse basing options closer to the Chinese mainland simply cannot be assumed under current conditions. Second, to be effective in striking hardened targets, the proposed missile would need to be highly accurate. Thus, we could expect that a Pershing III may be more expensive than a reconstituted Pershing II because of the demands for greater range and accuracy. Finally, while the technological and military-industrial capacity of the United States should be capable of developing such a system, the long period of inactivity in this area of research and development likely would add to the costs of the program. The Pershing IIIs would be expected to be road-mobile, or perhaps placed in hardened silos to maintain their survivability. On the already cramped Anderson Air Force Base on Guam, it is not immediately clear which configuration would be preferred in terms of feasibility and cost-effectiveness. So while these new missiles would certainly enhance the firepower that could be delivered on key Chinese targets, such as air bases, command and control nodes, critical military infrastructure,

---

[33] Stephen I. Schwartz, ed., *Atomic Audit: The Costs and Consequences of U.S. Nuclear Weapons since 1940*, Washington: Brookings Institution Press, 1998.

[34] Shlapak et al., 2009, p. 133.

and potentially China's missile forces, they are likely to be relatively costly in the intermediate term.

Assessing the Case for U.S. Land-Based Intermediate-Range Conventional Missiles

Some experts who have considered the problem of China's missiles view an "in-kind" U.S. response involving the deployment of land-based, intermediate-range conventional missiles as a particularly effective response:

> ...[W]ith its tactical fighter bases and surface ships increasingly vulnerable, the United States also may have no choice but to abrogate the [INF] treaty and deploy mobile land-based missiles—a capability much more difficult for China to attack—to places such as Japan; this could become the only way to deter Chinese aggression.[35]

In the view of these experts, these weapons would provide specific capabilities that would allow the United States to more effectively address the growing challenge of Chinese AA/AD capabilities. They view the U.S deployment of land-based intermediate-range missiles in East Asia as offering four distinct but related benefits. First, land-based intermediate-range conventional ballistic missiles are particularly suited to address the threat of China's short- and intermediate-range missile systems. Second, new U.S. conventional INF missiles are a necessary (and perhaps sufficient) component of U.S. capabilities required to deter China from launching a potential first-strike by holding critical targets at risk. Third, U.S. land-based intermediate-range conventional ballistic missiles are actually less escalatory than other potential U.S. responses that may be utilized in the event of a conflict and thus could contribute to crisis stability. Fourth, with access to available bases in the region, the deployment of U.S. mis-

---

[35] Mark Stokes and Dan Blumenthal, "Why China's Missiles Matter to Us," *Atlanta Journal-Constitution*, January 5, 2011.

siles would significantly complicate current Chinese plans and perhaps transform the existing and growing imbalance confronting the United States.

Land-based, intermediate-range conventional missiles are particularly effective for addressing the challenge of China's missile buildup.
Though experts are somewhat vague in articulating the precise military rationale underlying the view that intermediate-range conventional missiles are particularly effective means to address China's expanding missile forces, the argument seems to hinge on three key points:

- Given the current threats to forward-deployed U.S. aircraft, conventional land-based IRBMs would maintain or enhance U.S. firepower because of the greater penetrability and survivability of the missile system even in the event of an attack.
- Because of their powerful high-explosive conventional warhead and accuracy, these missiles could hold high-value targets, including airbases, missile installations and support infrastructure, and command and control assets, at risk in the face of China's improving air defenses and even in the event of a coordinated Chinese first strike.
- Beyond their ability to strike fixed targets under conflict conditions, these experts seem to also consider land-based conventional IRBMs suited for striking mobile targets, particularly Chinese missile launchers because of their speed and accuracy. The United States, "without its own intermediate-range missiles, must counter enemy missile systems with air raids—a very ineffective means."[36]

Historically, even with air superiority, the United States has had difficulties in effectively destroying mobile targets.[37] In a Taiwan conflict scenario, these experts argue that two factors would exacerbate this problem. First, the United States is unlikely to achieve air supe-

---

[36] Ryan, 2007.

[37] Alan Vick et al., *Aerospace Operations Against Elusive Ground Targets,* Santa Monica, Calif.: RAND Corporation, MR-1398-AF, 2001.

riority over Chinese coastal areas or the Taiwan Straits early in the conflict. Second, initial Chinese missile strikes on U.S. forward bases may degrade U.S. sortie rates and limit the capabilities that would contribute to an effective counterattack. In the view of these experts, with the penetration and survivability of U.S. tactical aircraft in question, U.S. land-based intermediate-range ballistic missiles seem to provide a unique capability that overcomes both of those potential drawbacks, allowing the United States to hold high-value, fixed, and mobile targets (particularly missile Transporter Erector Launchers, or TELs) at risk even in the event of an attack. As one expert says: "To deter a first strike, or to attack intermediate-range missile launchers after they fire and before they relocate, a nation needs its own intermediate-range missiles."[38]

These arguments in support of a land-based intermediate-range ballistic missile seem plausible, but they overlook several key points. First, ballistic missiles are not the only systems with attributes of high survivability and penetrability. As discussed above, standoff munitions like the Tactical Tomahawk LACM or the extended range JASSM fired from platforms like the Ohio-Class SSGN or B-1 bomber, respectively, would score relatively well on both dimensions. Second, while they are incapable of delivering the same quantity of high explosive as an IRBM, advanced U.S. cruise missiles are highly accurate. Perhaps being utilized in greater numbers than a ballistic missile would make them sufficient for striking fixed high-value targets. Finally, while ballistic missiles indeed may possess the survivability and penetrability to hold fixed targets at risk, it is not clear that they are capable of effectively addressing mobile or re-locatable targets. This is in large part because the attributes of the any given missile are only one component of an effective capability to detect and destroy mobile missile systems.

Detecting and destroying mobile targets such as missile TELs are dependent not only on the speed of the missile, but also (and perhaps more importantly) on the ability to detect mobile targets and battlefield awareness, or intelligence preparation of the battlespace (IPB), which ultimately will determine whether the United States will be able

---

[38] Ryan, 2007.

to locate and discern targets in the event of a conflict.[39] In large part, then, this is a question of C4ISR rather than the munitions delivered to the target. The speed of a ballistic missile may be preferable to a cruise missile, but ultimately the platform in question would also have to possess the ability to be retargeted and updated consistently throughout its flight by C4ISR assets in the theater.

> To defeat mobile missiles, the United States will need to acquire the ability to constantly monitor vehicle traffic and TEL launch activities and deliver weapons many hundreds of kilometers inside China. Given these requirements, the engagement concepts…rely on stealthy UAVs, satellites, and unattended ground sensors to detect and recognize TELs, and hypersonic standoff missiles to destroy the TELs.[40]

Despite the best efforts of the United States to harden and enhance its C4ISR capabilities in the Western Pacific, it seems somewhat unlikely that, in the event of a conflict, U.S. assets will not be degraded by Chinese activities. In the event that the United States is able to maintain its C4ISR network in the region, a deployment of U.S. conventional IRBMs to Guam is unlikely to arrive on time precisely because of the distance the missile must travel. Shorter-range ballistic missiles within 1,000 km may be capable of executing an anti-TEL mission, but it seems unlikely that those with a range of 3,500-4,000 km would be effective, given the distance and time it would have to travel and the need for extensive updating and re-targeting capabilities.[41] Advanced U.S. cruise missiles such as the Tactical Tomahawk currently possess these capabilities, and with improvements in speed and the ability to loiter over conflict areas, they may prove even more useful than ballistic missiles in this role.

---

[39] Vick et al., 2001, pp. 66–76.

[40] Ibid., p. 66.

[41] It would likely take 17 to 20 minutes for an intermediate-range ballistic missile to travel that distance. I am indebted to Markus Schiller for explaining the calculations behind this point. A cruise missile with the ability to loiter in a contested area and receive updates from C4ISR assets may provide a more cost-effective solution to this challenge.

Moreover, given the sheer number of Chinese missiles, the potential quantities of U.S. intermediate-range missiles that would be required to effectively address the mobile-missile role would be quite large. As discussed above, it has been estimated that a baseline requirement of approximately 600 ballistic missiles would be required to sufficiently target 40 Chinese airbases that would likely contribute to an attack on Taiwan.[42] But the quantities necessary to address mobile missiles would be significantly greater:

> The programmatic and political implications of this concept cannot be ignored. If the United States wanted the capability to launch waves of missiles against Chinese bases, or wanted the option to employ the weapon against other targets in China (for example, SRBM bases) many more than 600 missiles would be required. To protect them against preemptive attack, a survivable basing mode, such as hardened silos would be needed, adding to the costs.[43]

The costs associated with such a program would be significant—much greater than the $12 billion baseline estimate made above. And even with a highly accurate, perhaps re-targetable, stealthy, high-end ballistic missile, it is unclear that the "anti-TEL" mission is achievable without complete, real-time battlefield awareness, which the United States is unlikely to possess in the event of a conflict with China. This is particularly true if China is able to execute a well-coordinated first strike.

Considering other missions beyond the location and destruction of China's mobile missiles, the capacity remains essential to deliver munitions to important hardened fixed targets such as air bases, command and control installations, C4ISR nodes, and other military infrastructure. Despite the attractiveness of ballistic missiles for this mission, other munitions may be capable of assuming this role and providing the requisite firepower to degrade China's ability to coordi-

---

[42] Shlapak et al., 2009.

[43] Ibid., p. 133.

nate and conduct air operations across the Taiwan Straits and within the First Island Chain.

> Other concepts that exploit existing or programmed systems to suppress PLAAF sortie generation may be possible; for example, extended range JASSM missiles could be fired from USAF bombers against at least some Chinese targets. While less survivable than ballistic missiles, the stealthy JASSM should be more able to penetrate Chinese air defenses than TLAMs.[44]

Given existing assets such as the SSGN and fleet of B-1 bombers, the United States possesses the ability to deliver significant quantities of standoff munitions to fixed targets in the event of a conflict. Maintaining adequate stocks of existing weapon systems such as the Tactical Tomahawk land attack cruise missiles, as well as the development of the JASSM-ER, could leverage the capabilities of existing platforms while policymakers devise plans to maintain or enhance these capabilities over the longer term. One implied programmatic tradeoff that seems to emerge from this discussion is that higher-end solutions like a land-based, intermediate-range ballistic missile which are likely to be procured at relatively low quantities because of costs may not always be preferable to cruise missiles and other lower-end systems, which can be procured in high quantities and utilized in a variety of ways. Among those ways are high-volume saturation attacks that are likely to present real challenges to Chinese planners, despite the existing imbalance in ballistic missiles.

U.S. land-based intermediate range missiles are required to effectively deter China.

In enhancing its ability to hold key Chinese targets at risk, some experts seem to imply that deployment of U.S. theater missiles would significantly improve the U.S. ability to deter China in the event of a crisis. Acknowledging that the expansion of China's missile forces significantly undermines that potential contribution of theater missile defenses, an "in-kind" response by the United States that threatens to

---

[44] Ibid., p. 134.

hold Chinese missiles and related targets at risk is the only available option.

> Defending against sophisticated ballistic and ground-launched cruise missiles is extremely difficult....The only real defense against these weapons is offense, so countries threatened by China's missiles will seek to target the infrastructure supporting missile launchers within nuclear-armed China.[45]

While this traditional deterrence logic is generally applicable, it overstates the perceived contribution of land-based, intermediate-range missiles. This argument seems to assume that only a visible deployed (versus assumed or implied) capability is necessary to adequately signal U.S. resolve and underscore its commitment to defend Taiwan.[46] Given China's perceived commitment to opacity and ambiguity in its own nuclear deterrent posture, this seems a curious quality to attribute to Beijing's leadership.[47] It is unclear that Beijing would need a further signal of U.S. commitment. While China is indeed likely to view a new conventionally-armed, land-based, intermediate-range ballistic missile as threatening, U.S. strategic assets such as penetrating or stand-off bombers or cruise missile submarines would not be insufficient to signal U.S. commitment to defend Taiwan and deter China in the event of a crisis. Given declared U.S. policy, and its significant forward-based capabilities in the region, it is not obvious why Beijing would view the nature of the U.S. deterrent commitments as anything but robust. In fact, precisely because of the targeted nature of China's modernization programs, which seem predicated on effectively responding to a Taiwan crisis and undermining the capability of the United States or other states to intervene, there is some reason to believe that Beijing takes the U.S. commitment very seriously. Whether an imbalance in

---

[45] Stokes and Blumenthal, 2011.

[46] Lynn E. Davis, "Lessons of the INF Treaty," *Foreign Affairs,* Vol. 66, 1987-88.

[47] Lora Saalman, "How Chinese Analysts View Arms Control, Disarmament, and Nuclear Deterrence after the Cold War," in *Engaging China and Russia on Nuclear Disarmament,* eds. Cristina Hansell and William C. Potter, Monterey: James Martin Center for Nonproliferation Studies, 2009.

one set of capabilities would, over time, lead China to take more risks in coercing Taiwan is an important question. However, it is unclear that the deployment of highly effective U.S. counterforce capabilities is necessary to effectively signal American resolve.

As discussed above, while the current capabilities of the U.S. long-range bomber force may be in need of expansion, a mix of penetrating and standoff platforms, perhaps with a new lingering unmanned component, can certainly deliver the firepower necessary to the theater to deter—or, if necessary, effectively respond to—a potential conflict.[48] The deployment of U.S. bombers to the region can be a powerful signal of U.S. resolve in the event of a crisis. Similarly, the deployment of U.S. Navy assets, whether they are in the form of carrier task forces or submarines, can significantly enhance the capabilities available in the event of a crisis in a relatively short period of time. The deployment of Ohio-class submarines was viewed as sending just such a signal that the United States has the ability to "ramp up" its capabilities in the region when necessary. Obviously, in the absence of a crisis, if China launched a "bolt from the blue" attack, the opportunity to send such signals would not exist. However, in such a coordinated, first-strike scenario, the limited deployment of U.S. theater missiles likely would be a primary target of Chinese forces, and their ability to retaliate could be significantly degraded. With advance warning, new U.S. intermediate-range missiles may contribute to responding to such an attack, but it is not clear that their contribution would deter or prove decisive in defending against such an attack.

More generally, the implication that the deployment of U.S. land-based intermediate-range missiles would fundamentally alter the calculations of Chinese leaders seems to conflate the likely impact of conventional and nuclear missiles. The perception of land-based, intermediate-range missiles as a "game changer" seems more appropriate to nuclear-armed missiles that could truly threaten to destroy high-value targets in extremely short periods of time. Conventional ballistic missiles are still relatively limited in their overall military utility. As China clearly has shown, these weapons are actually needed in large quanti-

---

[48] Gunzinger, 2010.

ties to threaten the levels of damage to contribute to effective military operations. At a more basic level, experts that support a land-based, intermediate-range missile program are advocating for an improvement of the conventional military balance across the Taiwan Strait. As discussed above, however, this can be accomplished with other programs, and the introduction of land-based, intermediate-range conventional missiles may not prove to be worth the considerable cost.

In the event of a crisis, the existence of deployed U.S. intermediate-range missiles would be less escalatory than other potential U.S. responses.

In improving U.S. conventional capabilities and providing a clearly visible program that directly targets China's most threatening capabilities, experts in favor of the deployment of land-based intermediate-range conventional ballistic missile forces imply that such a deployment ostensibly contributes to improving crisis stability by decreasing the perceived benefits of a Chinese first strike. This is a dubious claim, and if a U.S. deployment was limited to Guam, first-strike incentives actually would increase, undermining crisis stability. At the same time, the implication that theater systems, because they are visible and expected to be used in a conflict, are inherently less escalatory than other possible U.S. responses is also questionable. Nevertheless, experts who support a potential U.S. IRBMs deployed in the region seem to imply that they are less likely to spur escalation than U.S. "central" strategic responses in event of conflict:

> If Washington remains bound by the INF, its response options in a conflict with China are highly escalatory. If U.S. tactical fighter bases and surface ships were hit by Chinese missiles, Washington would have to consider responding by targeting missile assets inside China with intercontinental ballistic missiles. To do so, Washington will need to further develop its Prompt Global Strike system, a means of accurately launching long-range missiles from the continental U.S. Because such missiles could also be used to carry nuclear weapons, Chinese defenders would have no way of knowing if the munitions flying toward them were carrying

nuclear or conventional warheads. This uncertainty raises the risk of a Chinese nuclear response.[49]

The problem with this logic is that U.S. IRBMs would seemingly target the same Chinese assets as any tactical or central strategic systems. Under almost any scenario that involved an attack on U.S. naval assets or bases in the region, U.S. forces would target systems that are almost exclusively located in mainland China, including airbases, TELs, and command and control installations. Once U.S. forces hit targets in mainland China, it is difficult to be confident about controlling escalation. Whether U.S. theater missiles, munitions from penetrating bombers, or submarine-launched missiles hit those targets, escalatory dynamics should be considered to be in effect. The assumption that theater forces are inherently less escalatory is dubious.

In fact, "central" U.S. strategic forces actually may be far less escalatory and inherently stabilizing in the event of a political crisis. Bomber forces can be deployed to a region, placed on alert, and ultimately recalled if necessary. Similarly, submarine-launched munitions can provide a highly controlled, graduated response. Barring a dramatic technological breakthrough in China's ASW capabilities, the U.S. submarine force remains a potent asset for responding to a conflict. Both the air and sea legs of the traditional triad are highly survivable and obviate the pressures to "use or lose" inherent in a vulnerable theater missile force. Obviously, ICBMs would be seen as highly escalatory, but would seem to be outside of consideration for most plausible scenarios involving the defense of Taiwan. Air- and sea-based assets that further expand the U.S. stand-off capabilities would seems to be both preferable from a crisis stability and military effectiveness point of view.

The United States will have access to bases to deploy land-based, intermediate-range missiles.

Finally, experts who support the deployment of U.S. land-based, intermediate-range missiles assume that with adequate basing options,

---

[49] Stokes and Blumenthal, 2011.

the United States will present a diversified threat to China's missile forces that will rectify the perceived imbalance in conventional forces. Depending on the nature of the eventual deployment, a Pershing III land-based intermediate-range conventional missile would indeed confront China with a vulnerability to be addressed in subsequent planning. It would need to commit resources that would ostensibly limit the capabilities that it could dedicate to other targets, such as U.S. forward bases or other assets in the region. Moreover, if the deployment of U.S. conventional IRBMs was significantly large and diversified at bases around the region, Chinese planners could not expect to execute any attack without sustaining significant damage. Such a scenario may indeed alter the balance in the region in a significant way. However, this is predicated on the assumption that regional bases will be available to host U.S. missile forces. This is simply unrealistic. In the absence of a major shift in Chinese policy that dramatically rejects its current "peaceful rise" to a more objectively aggressive and expansionist approach, the United States is unlikely to find bases beyond its own territories in the Western Pacific.

The nature of East Asian regional politics will be assessed in more depth in the next chapter, in the context of response to a U.S. withdrawal from the INF Treaty, but a couple of points are important to address. First, as the experience of the late 1970s reflects, regional allies are likely to oppose requests to host counterforce weapons that will target China.[50] Given the high levels of economic interdependence in the East Asian region and the central role that China has assumed in regional trade, countries such as Japan and South Korea are unlikely to view the threat of a Taiwan conflict as necessitating what would be viewed as a provocative response to a threat that only indirectly affects their security. Deploying missiles that directly target China on their territory would fundamentally alter the relationships between these states and, in turn, make them priority targets of China's offensive weapons. Even in the event of a significant erosion of regional diplo-

---

[50] Gerhard Wetting, "The Last Soviet Offensive in the Cold War: Emergence and Development of the Campaign against NATO Euromissiles, 1979-1983," *Cold War History,* Vol. 9, No. 1, 2009.

matic relations precipitated by a shift in Chinese diplomacy, domestic public opinion is likely to continue to oppose such deployments precisely because of the high likelihood of being pulled into in a future conflict. Thus the assumption that the United States would have multiple basing options that would allow for a significant diversification of missile forces is thus highly problematic, and any prudent planning for developing such a program should assume that deployment would be limited to U.S. territories. This fact alone significantly undermines the case for U.S. conventional IRBMs as a response to China's missile programs. An inability to access bases will affect costs by increasing the range requirements, and the likely limited nature of the deployment removes many of the perceived strategic or operational benefits that such a larger-scale, diversified deployment could offer.

Potential Implications of a U.S. Conventional INF Missile Deployment

In order to consider and assess the potential larger implications of a U.S. withdrawal from the INF Treaty or cooperative alteration of the Treaty to allow for the development and deployment of new IRBMs in the Pacific region, the literature on China's strategy and doctrine provides a basis for analysis.[51] Specifically, the significant shift in China's notion of "Local War Under High Technology Conditions," which has shaped much of China's policies and behavior over the past decade, would logically inform Beijing's response. One key concept that influences the subsequent analysis is that a central component of China's recent strategy has been to effectively construct a buffer from U.S. pre-

---

[51] See for example Cliff et al., 2007; Stuart E. Johnson and Duncan Long, eds., *Coping with the Dragon: Essays of PLA Transformation and the U.S. Military,* Washington: National Defense University, 2007; James C. Mulvenon and David Finklestein, eds., *China's Revolution in Doctrinal Affairs: Emerging Trends in the Operational Art of the Chinese People's Liberation Army,* Washington: CNA Corporation, 2005; Mulvenon et al., 2006; Michael Pillsbury, *China Debates the Future Security Environment,* Honolulu: University Press of the Pacific, 2004; Michael Pillsbury, ed., *Chinese Views of Future Warfare,* Honolulu: University Press of the Pacific, 2002.

cision-guided munitions (PGMs) and create what is essentially defense-in-depth. This objective seemingly has been an important tenet of China's strategy derived from Beijing's lessons learned from the U.S. response to the 1996 Taiwan Crisis, the two Gulf Wars, and the U.S. air campaign against Serbia.[52] Pushing the United States beyond the first, and eventually, second island chains contributes to this objective, and provides China with a measure of insulation from U.S. attack in the event of a crisis. An important open question is whether China views attacks on U.S. forward bases on allied soil as crossing a critical threshold that would increase the probability of escalation to direct attacks on the Chinese mainland. Nonetheless, the deployment of U.S. IRBMs would certainly undermine this important strategic objective; it would place the mainland directly at risk and remove the perceived advantages China has created with its modernization program.

Beyond its substantial program costs, a deployment of U.S. land-based intermediate-range conventional ballistic missiles likely would have significant political and military implications for the U.S.-China relationship. First, in withdrawing from the INF Treaty, the United States would likely have to identify the threat to its "supreme interests" that has driven its decision. It will be difficult to do so without singling out China as that primary threat. Moreover, the actual deployment of a highly capable, intermediate-range conventional missile aimed at high-value Chinese targets is likely to be interpreted as highly provocative, and is likely to transform China's perception of a threat from the United States. Second, the deployment of what are perceived as highly effective U.S. missiles on Guam would likely decrease crisis stability, placing pressure on both China and the United States in the event of a crisis. Finally, while withdrawal from the INF Treaty and deployment of land-based, intermediate-range ballistic missiles are both driven by the perceived need to address the expansion of China's missile force,

[52] Andrew S. Erickson and David D. Yang, "Using the Land to Control the Sea?: Chinese Analysts Consider the Antiship Ballistic Missile," *Naval War College Review,* Vol. 62, No. 4, 2009; Robert S. Ross, "The 1995-96 Taiwan Strait Confrontation: Coercion, Credibility, and the Use of Force," *International Security,* Vol. 25, No. 2, 2000; Robert S. Ross, "Navigating the Taiwan Strait: Deterrence, Escalation Dominance, and U.S.-China Relations," *International Security,* Vol. 27, No. 2, 2002.

it is unclear that China would respond by limiting its own deployments. If the U.S. missiles are viewed as particularly threatening to Chinese forces, it would be expected that China may actually expand its intermediate-range missile forces well beyond current levels, ultimately limiting the perceived improvement in the balance that the U.S. deployment initially achieved.

Transforming China's Threat Perception

The most straightforward effect of a U.S. withdrawal from the INF would be to increase Chinese mistrust of U.S. intentions. As experts have written elsewhere, China's limited nuclear deterrent, including its commitment to a No First Use (NFU) doctrine, and focused military modernization, has been targeted toward averting nuclear blackmail and deterring what Beijing perceives as interference in its development and peaceful rise.[53] The opaque nature of China's policymaking apparatus has complicated efforts to understand China's ultimate long-term objectives, and China's assertion of exclusive rights in the South China Sea and territorial disputes with Japan have contributed to this uncertainty.[54]

What seems clear, at least in the short term, is that the focus of China's military modernization has been predicated on deterring outside intervention in a Taiwan conflict, and improving its ability to prevail should deterrence fail. The central challenge of U.S. policy on China is balancing cooperation and conflict as well as hedging against the emergence of an aggressive China as it continues to consolidate its power and expand its material capabilities. While deterring China from coercing its neighbors and following the provocative path of historical rising powers, it is also important to avoid engaging in policies that lead to a self-fulfilling prophecy and contribute to the emergence of a belligerent and revisionist China. In fact, given the current rela-

---

[53] Lora Saalman, *China & the U.S. Nuclear Posture Review*, Washington: Carnegie Endowment for International Peace, 2011.

[54] Peter Hays Gries, "Problems of Misperception in U.S.-China Relations," *Orbis*, Vol. 53, No. 2, 2009; Evan S. Medeiros, *China's International Behavior: Activism, Opportunism, and Diversification*, Santa Monica, Calif.: RAND Corporation, MG-850-AF, 2009.

tions between the two states, it is difficult to see the political impetus for such a policy decision in the absence of a prior deterioration of U.S.-China relations to the point at which the probability of conflict has increased, and the perceived gap in U.S. missile forces is perceived as an immediate and acute threat warranting such a controversial diplomatic response.

Under current conditions, the withdrawal of the United States from the INF Treaty thus likely would severely undermine relations with the People's Republic of China, particularly if the rationale of the United States included some direct reference to China's missile forces. As discussed above, the protocol for withdrawing from the treaty mandates that the abrogating party is expected to present reasons for doing so. While such a rationale likely will be couched in broad diplomatic language, it will be difficult to explain the U.S. objectives without an implicit acknowledgement of the role of China's expanding capabilities as the overriding threat to the United States. Given current trends, the U.S. withdrawal from the INF likely would be viewed with great concern in Beijing and would seemingly exacerbate Chinese mistrust of U.S. intentions. The actual plan to exploit the new freedom of a post-INF environment and develop and deploy new missile systems in the East Asian theater directed at Chinese mainland targets is likely to be perceived as highly escalatory, and could perhaps even precipitate a diplomatic crisis. Given current trends, Beijing seemingly would view as highly escalatory the withdrawal from the INF Treaty and a decision to deploy land-based missile systems in East Asia Though the United States' intention may indeed be to compensate for a perceived gap in U.S. deterrent capabilities and the vulnerability of forward-based assets in the region, thus ostensibly improving stability and decreasing the probability of conflict, it is doubtful that Beijing would view U.S. deployments as merely addressing a gap in capabilities.

Potential for Crisis Instability, First-Strike Incentives, and Escalation
Depending on the nature of the missile systems that are developed and deployed, U.S. policymakers should expect China to view the deployments as highly threatening and provocative. Considering the history of the "dual-track" decision in Western Europe in 1979, the Soviet per-

ceptions of the deployment of Pershing IIs was that the United States was attempting to alter the balance between NATO and the Warsaw Pact, not simply to offset the deployment of Soviet SS-20s.[55]

Given the missiles' ability to hit Russian targets with little warning time, Moscow viewed the deployment as highly escalatory, and it intensified the deterioration of relations between the United States and Soviet Union in the early 1980s.[56] In the absence of general deterioration of U.S.-China relations to something approaching a diplomatic shift to "contain" China, the introduction of a Pershing III missile on Guam could be expected to spur a similar reaction from China. A highly capable missile that could destroy command and control assets, missile launchers, and other high-value targets would be seen as a highly threatening, albeit conventional, "counterforce" weapon. Thus, we should expect that these weapons would be perceived at the very least as important targets in the event of a crisis. This leads to two dynamics that could undermine crisis stability and introduce first-strike incentives.

First, if the United States is limited in its deployment of new land-based, intermediate-range ballistic missiles to Guam, the simple fact of their consolidated position in a relatively small geographic area creates a vulnerability, whether they are mobile or in hardened silos. China is presented with a limited, fixed target that potentially could be significantly degraded or knocked out in the event of an effective, coordinated first strike. Thus, in a political crisis, leaders in Beijing would have preventive motives to attack U.S. missile deployments to remove the most threatening assets from the U.S. arsenal. The second, related dynamic arises from U.S. knowledge of these Chinese motives. Because there are pressures for China to preventively attack Guam, the United States finds itself in a position to "use or lose" its missile forces as a diplomatic crisis intensifies. Knowing that they may be the targets of a Chinese first strike, pressures would build upon the United States

---

[55] David Holloway, *The Soviet Union and the Arms Race,* New Haven: Yale University Press, 1984.

[56] Arnav Manchanda, "When Truth Is Stranger Than Fiction: The Able Archer Incident," *Cold War History,* Vol. 9, No. 1, 2009.

to consider striking first out of fear that the probabilities of surviving a Chinese first strike are low and that seizing the initiative would improve the probability of success.

In either case, the potential for miscalculations and even accidental exchanges would increase, as forces on high alert seek to avoid being caught off guard. Similarly, the pressures to "use or lose" may contribute to inadvertent escalation, as the fear of suffering a disarming or degrading first strike would pressure leaders to utilize all available munitions. As discussed above, escalation dynamics should be considered in effect once targets on the Chinese mainland are hit. This would be expected fairly early on in any conceivable conflict scenario.

Altering China's Missile-Centric Strategy[57]

Finally, a more basic point inherent in the logic of deploying theater missiles is that a buildup and even perhaps long-term diversification of those forces will alter China's cost calculus in planning for a Taiwan operation. The United States can create more targets and deploy greater capabilities within the theater and at some level, but it is far from clear that such assets will deter China. China's modernization, focused on an expansion of missile forces, seems to reflect a different cost-effectiveness calculus from that of the United States. Traditional U.S. reliance on tactical and strategic airpower is premised on the straightforward concept that missiles can only be used once, whereas airpower is a much more versatile (reusable) capability. Nonetheless, China's development and procurement priorities are unlikely to be fundamentally altered by what likely would be a limited U.S. deployment of theater missiles. Engaging China in a missile race, in which it seems China has a comparative quantitative advantage (and perhaps a qualitative advantage, at least in the short-to-medium term) does not necessarily seem to prove cost-effective for the United States.

Rather than responding to the asymmetry created by China's missile-centric modernization program with an "in-kind response," it would seem prudent for the United States to leverage areas in which it may possess comparative advantages, such as undersea, surface, and

---

[57] Mulvenon et al., 2006.

airpower operations as discussed above. More basically, given the asymmetry of interests that exists in the Taiwan crisis scenario, it is unlikely that the United States is ever going to be able to completely overcome China's "home field" advantage in military terms. Given the centrality of averting Taiwan's independence to China's national interests, it should be expected Beijing will commit whatever resources necessary to maximize its probability of prevailing in a conflict. As written elsewhere, this does not entail a general war with the United States, but a limited-aims conflict in which China has distinct geographic advantages, bolstered by its military modernization program.[58]

We already have witnessed this challenge in considering U.S. theater ballistic missile defenses in the region, where it is highly unlikely (or prohibitively costly) that the United States could acquire and deploy active defense capable of defending critical targets, or even offsetting Chinese plans, in the event of a conflict. In short, a deployment of U.S. intermediate range missiles that represented only a marginal improvement over these capabilities (because of limits on basing and costs) is unlikely to alter Chinese considerations. It may, in fact, only prove self-defeating if China ultimately compensates for U.S. improvements with a further expansion of missile forces.

Conclusion

China's missile expansion creates a serious threat to U.S. interests. However, it is not clear that the U.S. development and deployment of land-based intermediate-range conventional missiles, currently prohibited under the INF Treaty, would represent the optimal means of addressing that threat. While a Pershing III IRBM would enhance the conventional capabilities that U.S. forces could utilize in the event a conflict, it would be costly. Alternative programs may provide similar capabilities, while proving more cost-effective and operationally flexible.

---

[58] Cliff et al., 2007; Hoyler, 2010.

Despite arguments in favor of such a weapon, a U.S. land-based IRBM is unlikely to prove useful in effectively targeting Chinese mobile missiles. While it could contribute to striking important fixed targets, other munitions and platforms may be capable of executing this mission. It is unclear that the visibility of the deployment of new U.S. missiles in the theater would have any greater effect of deterring China than existing U.S. platforms that can be moved into the region in the event of a crisis. Nor is it obvious that land-based, intermediate-range conventional ballistic missiles would be less escalatory than "central" U.S. systems. Finally, the United States is unlikely to find access to bases in the region beyond U.S. territories such as Guam, which greatly increases the costs and limits the perceived contributions of land-based, intermediate-range conventional missiles. At the same time, the deployment of these missiles likely would have significant implications for the U.S.-China relationship, significantly increasing China's perception of the threat posed by the United States, decrease crisis stability, and potentially spurring further Chinese expansion and an arms race that could ultimately leave the United States worse off. On balance, a Pershing-III land-based, intermediate-range conventional ballistic missile likely would be costly and make only a limited military contribution, while the larger implications of its deployment are worrisome.

The next chapter will examine the potential political and security implications of withdrawing from the INF Treaty, which would be necessary for the United States to develop and deploy the Pershing-III. These costs, too, are likely to be significant and far-reaching, further undermining the case for a new land-based intermediate-range missile in response to China's military modernization.

CHAPTER FIVE

Political/Military Implications of a U.S. Withdrawal from the INF Treaty

This chapter considers the potential responses to a U.S. withdrawal from, or the cooperative dissolution of the INF Treaty by the United States and Russia. Specifically, it will examine the likely reactions of Russia, NATO, and U.S. allies in East Asia. Finally, the impact of a U.S. withdrawal from the INF Treaty will be considered in the context of the larger objective of global nonproliferation and the MTCR. While prediction in any field is difficult, the analysis presented here is built upon a rigorous evaluation of objective regional expertise of RAND and other such organizations, as well as government documents, media accounts, and interviews with regional and policy experts. The objective of this chapter is to focus on several major key considerations in each setting to present a basic picture of what can be expected in the event of a U.S. withdrawal. Building upon the likely reactions of key states to a U.S. withdrawal from the INF Treaty, the chapter examines whether the nature of the withdrawal (unilateral or cooperative) and working closely with Russia, as well as the likely affected allies and friends, would significantly alter the potential political and security implications discussed. Finally, the chapter considers whether the INF Treaty could be revised to either allow both the United States and Russia conventional, land-based intermediate-range ballistic and cruise missiles, or to set geographic limitations for the deployment of conventional or nuclear INF missile forces by each nation.

A Framework for Assessing Political/Military Costs

Given the longevity of the INF Treaty and the complex and multifaceted nature of U.S. relations with various regional allies and partners, assessing the potential military and political costs of a U.S. withdrawal from the Treaty or a cooperative revision of the Treaty that significantly alters the existing status quo is a difficult task. This chapter will consider a set of relatively straightforward questions in an attempt to analyze the impact of such a change and draw out potential implications.

- How would the abrogation or transformation of the INF Treaty impact the security environments confronting critical U.S. allies in regional contexts?
- What impact would the potential deployment of U.S. or Russian IRBMs likely have on critical U.S. allies and partners? Specifically, how would the introduction of these systems alter existing regional security environments?
- Would allies view the U.S. deployment of IRBMs as contributing to a net improvement of their own security vis-à-vis potential common threats?
- These questions necessarily remain fairly general in scope, but they provide a means to distill key foreseeable implications of a significant change in the status quo associated with a dissolution or transformation of the INF Treaty.

Russia

In considering a U.S. withdrawal from the INF Treaty, Russia's is the first response that should be assessed. As the other signatory to the treaty, Russia remains constrained from the development of medium- and intermediate-range ballistic and cruise missiles carrying conventional or nuclear warheads. As discussed above, in 2007, Russian President Vladimir Putin publicly discussed withdrawing from the INF Treaty, arguing that it no longer served Russian national interests.[1] Given Russia's geography, the intermediate-range missile programs of countries such as China, India, North Korea, and Pakistan do constitute potential threats to its national territory. Moreover, under Putin and his successor Dmitry Medvedev, Russian foreign policy has generally been more assertive in exercising influence in its traditional "near abroad" (or the former Soviet space), as exemplified by the 2009 intervention in Georgia.[2] Deterring external intervention (or subversion or terrorism) in regions adjacent to Russia is an important security objective.[3] Intermediate-range missile forces would seem well suited to enhancing a deterrent posture in these regions and projecting power beyond them, but Moscow has resisted pulling out of the INF Treaty, relying on its strategic arsenal to provide a credible deterrent against potential threats.

One trend that has persisted since the end of the Cold War is the decline of Russia's conventional military forces.[4] As a result, nuclear weapons continue to play an important role in Russia's security policy.[5] In the early 1990s, Russia officially rescinded the No-First Use (NFU) doctrine that had defined Soviet doctrine during the Cold War, and as its conventional forces declined, the widespread perception emerged that Russia increasingly has relied on nuclear weapons, particularly non-strategic nuclear weapons (NSNW).[6] In its most recent Strategic Doctrine, 2010's "National Defense of Russia," the use of nuclear weap-

---

[1]   Tony Halpin, "Putin Confronts US with Threat to Arms Pact," *Times* (London), October 13, 2007.

[2]   Olga Oliker, Keith Crane, Lowell H. Schwartz, and Catherine Yusupov, *Russian Foreign Policy: Sources and Implications,* Santa Monica, Calif.: RAND Corporation, MG-768-AF, 2009.

[3]   Andrei Shleifer and Daniel Treisman, "Why Moscow Says No - a Question of Russian Interests, Not Psychology," *Foreign Affairs,* Vol. 90, No. 1, 2011.

[4]   Richard Boudreaux, "Russia's Fading Army Fights Losing Battle to Reform Itself," *Wall Street Journal,* April 20, 2011.

[5]   Vladimir Dvorkin, "Reducing Russia's Reliance on Nuclear Weapons in Security Policies," in *Engaging China and Russia on Nuclear Disarmament,* eds. Cristina Hansell and William C. Potter, Monterey: James Martin Center for Nonproliferation Studies, 2009.

[6]   Luke Champlin and Volha Charnysh, "Russia Plans Changes to Military Doctrine," *Arms Control Today,* December 2009.

ons is contemplated in response to a large-scale conventional attack that threatens the survival of the state as well as a potential nuclear attack.[7] This maintains a higher threshold than some experts had predicted, but does leave open the possibility of nuclear use to de-escalate conflicts against adversaries deemed to possess qualitatively superior conventional forces.[8] However, while nuclear weapons continue to play an important role, Putin and Medvedev have supported the long-term modernization of Russia's conventional military forces, and given the poor state of those forces, the investment required will be considerable. So while maintaining its nuclear capabilities at levels deemed necessary to deter, the expansion of those capabilities likely will be weighed carefully against the potential contribution to conventional modernization that would be lost.[9] Thus, in attempting to understand Russia's likely reactions to a removal of the restraints imposed by the INF Treaty, it is important to consider the context of current Russian Strategic Doctrine and the underlying tension between investments in nuclear and conventional forces.

Reasons to Agree

Because Moscow initially threatened to withdraw from the INF Treaty in the wake of U.S. decisions to deploy missile defense systems in Central Europe in 2007, it is not surprising that the U.S. withdrawal from the Treaty, either unilaterally or in cooperation with Russia, would be amenable to the Kremlin, at least according to public statements. While some commentators have argued that the threats to withdraw from INF were targeted for domestic political consumption, the freedom from INF Treaty restrictions would provide Russia with a capability that seems to be particularly well suited for its overall security policy.[10]

---

[7]   Nikolai Sokov, "The New, 2010 Russian Military Doctrine: The Nuclear Angle," Center for Nonproliferation Studies, February 5, 2010.

[8]   Volha Charnysh, "Russian Nuclear Threshold Not Lowered," *Arms Control Today,* March 2010.

[9]   Sokov, 2010.

[10]   "Is Russia Bluffing on Nuclear Treaty?" *Jane's Intelligence Digest*, October 29, 2007.

Considering the difficulties of reforming (if not rebuilding) its conventional military capabilities, nuclear weapons have assumed an important role in Russian doctrine. Given Russia's concerns for its traditional sphere of interest, its near abroad and the potential threat of outside states intervening in this region, INF missiles would seem to provide a useful contribution to an enhanced-deterrent capability— if even only as a "stop-gap" until conventional forces are improved.[11] Current short-range systems and tactical nuclear weapons are viewed as unable to reach targets that would be most likely to threaten Russian interests in its near abroad, such as Ukraine, Georgia, and much of Central Asia.[12] New INF missile programs would provide the capability to hold these potential threats at risk, greatly enhancing the Russian deterrent and ostensibly providing a significant capability to coerce states perceived as "interfering" in the affairs of Russia's neighbors.[13]

As for the technical capacity of Russia to exploit the newfound freedom that a post-INF would provide, some experts contend that theater-level missile programs seem to be an area of research and development in which Russia maintains a relatively robust capacity.[14] Russia has been successful in developing a new short-range missile system, the Iskander, and has also achieved success in the development of theater missile defense programs.[15] While it is not a given that Russia would immediately build a new INF missile system, and there has been some discussion as to whether it would be a technical or strategic priority in the short-term, the development of a new medium-range missile system is an achievable goal over the longer term.

Finally, but perhaps most importantly for the United States, a new generation of INF missiles would significantly offset what Russia

---

[11] Oliker et al., 2009, p. 174; Sokov, 2010.

[12] Miles Pomper, William Potter, and Nikolai Sokov, "Reducing Tactical Nuclear Weapons in Europe," *Survival,* Vol. 52, No. 1, 2010.

[13] Interviews conducted by the author, Washington, DC, April–May 2010.

[14] John Wood, *Russia, the Asymmetric Threat to the United States,* Santa Barbara: Praeger, 2009.

[15] David C. Isby, "Extended-Range Iskander Could Break INF Treaty," *Jane's Missiles & Rockets,* January 1, 2008.

has perceived as a major imbalance in conventional forces in Europe. Russia suspended its participation in the Conventional Forces Europe (CFE) treaty regime, seeking to alter the treaty to better address its security concerns.[16] Intermediate-range missiles such as the Cold War SS-20 would hold targets in Western Europe at risk and contribute to a much clearer deterrent to any NATO intervention in Moscow's western neighbors. Thus these systems are viewed with real military value to Moscow, even with a potential diplomatic price.

Reasons to Oppose

While the end of the INF Treaty would remove constraints on Russia to rebuild its intermediate-range missile capabilities, reasons remain for Russia to be concerned. Russia's misgivings about U.S. power are driven by the perception that it seeks maximum military capabilities and the flexibility to effectively intervene anywhere around the globe.[17] Despite its maintenance of the second-largest nuclear arsenal on the planet, the erosion of Russian conventional power is striking and is clearly understood in Russian policy circles. The perceived conventional superiority of the United States confronts Russian leaders with a major vulnerability.[18] This has ostensibly undermined the strategic balance between the United States and Russia, leaving Russia to resort to its nuclear arsenal, which also is now much smaller than that of the United States. Without the restraints of the INF Treaty, Russia may recover capabilities that allow it to better address current threats, but the United States also will be free to develop its own forces. The removal of INF prohibitions would present Russia with another area of potential competition with America, and Russian leaders are not ignorant of Europe's likely response to new Russian missiles. The potential return of U.S. intermediate-range missiles to NATO member countries in response to a Russian deployment is a highly threatening proposition.[19]

---

[16] "Russia Would Benefit from Leaving INF Treaty, Say Analysts," 2007.

[17] Arbatov, 2011.

[18] "Russia Would Benefit from Leaving INF Treaty, Say Analysts," 2007.

[19] Kislyakov, 2007.

Ultimately, the net result of a U.S. withdrawal, whether unilateral or cooperative, may not favor Russia, and military and political leaders seem to understand this. Moreover, while the freedom to deploy intermediate-range missiles may have some marginal improvement in Russia's security vis-à-vis its neighbors, it already possesses other means to deliver nuclear weapons in the event of a regional conflict, including air-launched cruise missiles, bombers, or even a Topol ICBM.[20] At a more basic level, a U.S. withdrawal from the INF Treaty would mark a dramatic reversal of the more cooperative policies of the Obama administration and the progress toward "resetting" the U.S.-Russia relationship as exemplified by the New START treaty.[21] Thus, while Russia might ostensibly welcome the freedom to utilize INF missiles in its strategic doctrine, the larger impact seems more complicated and potentially troubling for U.S.-Russia relations.[22]

Europe

The unilateral U.S. withdrawal or cooperative dissolution of the INF Treaty with Russia is likely to be most controversial in Europe, where it has visibly contributed to stability and security. Despite the recent reaffirmation that NATO remains a nuclear alliance so long as nuclear weapons exist, as articulated in the recent 2010 Strategic Concept, pressures in Western Europe have intensified to remove the remaining tactical or non-strategic nuclear weapons (NSNW) in NATO's arsenal. Prior to the Strategic Concept process, Germany, Holland, Belgium, the Netherlands, and Italy made a joint formal request to remove the

---

[20] Nikolai Sokov, "Military Exercises in Russia: Naval Deterrence Failures Compensated by Strategic Rocket Success," Monterey: James Martin Center for Nonproliferation Studies, February 24, 2004.

[21] David J. Kramer, "Resetting U.S.-Russian Relations: It Takes Two," *Washington Quarterly*, Vol. 33, No. 1, 2010.

[22] Interviews conducted by the author, Washington, DC, April–May 2010.

remaining 200 or so warheads from NATO bases.[23] Yet while Western European states view the deterrent value of tactical nuclear weapons as decreasing, NATO's newer Central European members take a less sanguine view of Russia and its increasing assertiveness.[24] Complicating matters, Germany seemingly has developed its own independent diplomatic approach to Russia.[25] Beneath all of this is a growing drift between Washington and Brussels, which has emerged in discussion of NATO contributions, to Afghanistan, and most recently the response to Libya.[26] Several European security experts emphasized this in a recent report:

> As neither a liability nor an asset, Europe has largely ceased to feature in American security accounts. Whoever is in charge in Washington, the two sides of the Atlantic will continue to find their views aligned on many, perhaps most, of the security challenges they face; but they will no longer do so as complementary parts of one unified, Euro-Atlantic community.[27]

Yet, despite differing perceptions of Russian intentions, a U.S. withdrawal from the INF Treaty that allowed Russia to possess and deploy a new generation of medium- and intermediate-range nuclear missiles would be perceived with great concern in Europe.

---

[23] Julian Borger, "Five NATO States to Urge Removal of US Nuclear Arms in Europe," *Guardian*, Feburary 23, 2010.

[24] Mark Landler, "U.S. to Resist NATO Push to Remove Tactical Arms," *International Herald Tribune*, April 23, 2010.

[25] Stephen F. Szabo, "Can Berlin and Washington Agree on Russia?," *Washington Quarterly*, Vol. 32, No. 4, 2009.

[26] Christopher Chivvis, *Recasting NATO's Strategic Concept: Possible Directions for the United States*, Santa Monica, Calif.: RAND Corporation, OP-280-AF, 2009; Andrew R. Hoehn and Sarah Harting, *Risking NATO: Testing the Limits of the Alliance in Afghanistan*, Santa Monica, Calif.: RAND Corporation, MG-974-AF, 2010.

[27] Ivan Krastev, Mark Leonard, Dimitar Bechev, Jana Kobzova, and Andrew Wilson, *The Spectre of a Multipolar Europe*, London: European Council on Foreign Relations, 2010, p. 59.

Reversing the Non-Nuclear Trend

Given current trends, the most problematic facet of a U.S. withdrawal from INF would be the dramatic reversal of policy that de-emphasizes nuclear weapons. Many NATO partners have strongly supported the Obama administration's commitment to arms control agreements and a more fundamental policy objective of moving toward a world without nuclear weapons.[28] While President Obama's Prague speech of April 18, 2009 came less than a decade after a Bush administration Nuclear Policy Review (NPR) that was widely perceived as lowering the threshold for nuclear use, it seems clear that many European leaders enthusiastically endorse the goal of "global zero" and are interested in facilitating progress toward that end, as the movement to reduce tactical nuclear weapons reflected.[29] While the connection is not entirely clear, it is difficult to see how a U.S. decision to unilaterally withdraw from INF would be not seen as "pulling out the rug" from under its NATO allies and significantly impeding the progress toward global zero.[30]

The Euro-Missile Crisis Redux

For NATO decisionmakers, a U.S. withdrawal from the INF Treaty will ostensibly set the stage for a new, unfettered modernization of Russian theater missile forces, which will present a clear threat to all of Europe. Yet even without any Russian declared policy to deploy new intermediate-range missiles, European leaders will be gravely concerned. Moreover, neither U.S. ballistic missile defense nor a commitment to return U.S. missiles are likely to provide the deterrent capability required to reassure European allies in the face of a renewed

---

[28] Alvaro de Vasconcelos and Marcin Zaborowski, eds., *European Perspectives on the New American Foreign Policy Agenda,* Paris: European Union Institute for Security Studies, 2009.

[29] Alvaro de Vasconcelos and Marcin Zaborowski, eds., *The Obama Moment: European and American Perspectives,* Paris: European Union Institute for Security Studies, 2009; Fitzpatrick, 2011; Claudine Lamond and Paul Ingram, "Politics around US Tactical Nuclear Weapons in European Host States," *BASIC Getting to Zero* Papers, No. 11.

[30] Interviews conducted by the author, Washington, DC, April–May 2010.

Russian threat.[31] While we would expect any decision to end the INF Treaty to be accompanied by extremely vigorous diplomatic campaigns to assuage the concerns of NATO allies, the dramatic transformation of the European security environment created by renewed Russian INF capabilities is unlikely to be satisfactorily addressed by any subsequent U.S. actions. The dissolution of the INF Treaty would seemingly be a major advantage to Russia, allowing it to improve its deterrent capabilities and its security unilaterally vis-à-vis a number of perceived threats, most importantly NATO.[32] The ability to hold all of Western Europe at risk would provide an enhanced deterrent against what Russia perceives as interference by outside power in territories considered to be within Russia's traditional sphere of influence. It also could again call into question the United States' extended deterrent guarantee.[33]

Old Europe vs. New Europe

Precisely because of the capabilities of a new generation of Russian theater missiles, divisions between NATOs founding Western European partners and the newer members of Central Europe could intensify and even push the alliance into crisis.[34] While Russia does not require the range of intermediate missiles to threaten NATO's newer members such as Poland, the Czech Republic, and Romania, the ability to hold Western Europe at risk could result in a split between the two groups and a clear breach of alliance solidarity. There already has been significant discussion about the credibility of Article V as NATO has expanded eastward, and a U.S.-instigated diplomatic initiative that harms NATO's interests and guarantees will be viewed with concern.[35] The decision to maintain tactical nuclear weapons was in large part predicated on maintaining alliance solidarity and addressing the con-

---

[31] Larrabee, 2008.

[32] Ivan Krastev et al., 2010.

[33] Ibid.

[34] James M. Goldgeier, "NATO's Future: Facing Old Divisions and New Threats," *Harvard International Review*, July 2009.

[35] Thomas Fedyszyn, "Saving NATO: Renunciation of the Article 5 Guarantee," *Orbis*, Vol. 54, No. 3, 2010.

cerns of Eastern members, despite the lack of domestic political support among Western partners.[36] Poland's support for a U.S. missile defense system will almost certainly make it a target of Russian missile forces, though short-range Iskander missiles are capable of executing that mission. Over the longer term, the potential for crisis between NATO and Russia over Ukraine or Georgia will necessitate a difficult balance between the differing threat perceptions of Western and Central Europe, complicating a unified position and undermining NATO's deterrent and its credibility as an alliance.[37]

NATO's Relevance to U.S. Security

The perception that the United States' primary rationale from withdrawing from the INF Treaty would be to redress the growing threat of Chinese missiles will be present significant problems for relations with Europe.[38] The notion that the United States would willingly abrogate the Treaty, and in so doing, create a potential for Russian development of capabilities that are highly threatening to Europe's security, will be received with concern. It may not be immediately clear that the security environment in Europe has changed. Russia may not embark on the development and deployment of new intermediate range missiles. However, the probability seems low that Russia would tacitly commit to the norms of the Treaty after a U.S. withdrawal. Given Russian concerns about NATO enlargement, and perceptions of European interference in regions traditionally considered part of Russia's "sphere of influence," it is difficult to envision Russia forgoing a visible capability to deter or coerce NATO members and address various other key regional threats.[39] Russian domestic politics at the time of the with-

---

[36] F. Stephen Larrabee and Christopher Chivvis, "Biden's Task in Eastern Europe: Reassurance," *Christian Science Monitor*, October 20, 2009; Dale McFeatters, "NATO Should Keep Nukes," *Korea Times*, April 26, 2010; Walter Pincus, "Panel Urges Keeping U.S. Nuclear Arms in Europe," *Washington Post*, January 9, 2009.

[37] Interviews conducted by the author, Washington, DC, April–May 2010.

[38] Ibid.

[39] Dmitri Trenin, "Russia's Spheres of Interest, Not Influence," *Washington Quarterly*, Vol. 32, No. 4, 2009.

drawal will certainly shape the ultimate response and the potential for a larger diplomatic crisis in Europe, and the perception of relations with NATO will play a central role. More generally, a U.S. withdrawal from the INF Treaty will call into question the U.S. commitment to Europe and the future of the Alliance.[40] It will be difficult to argue that the United States continues to view European interests as priorities, if the net result of a withdrawal from the Treaty is a significant increase in the uncertainty of the security environment in Europe and a potential increase in the vulnerability of Europe to Russian coercion.[41]

East Asia

Assuming the persistence of current trends, increasing economic integration and deepening trade relationships are likely to define interstate relations in the East Asia region, led by China's emergence as a global economic power and the major market for regional exporters.[42]

While historic tensions among the major regional powers remain unresolved and occasionally flare into diplomatic controversies, the likelihood of conflict in the region remains relatively low. Two obvious exceptions are provocations by the Democratic People's Republic of Korea (DPRK) and a potential conflict over Taiwan, and more recently territorial disputes in the South China Sea have intensified. More generally, Chinese military modernization has caused concerns in the region, and China's recent assertiveness has pushed states to restore ties with the United States to hedge against a future threat. However, China's targeted buildup often has been portrayed as being focused on a Taiwan contingency—an internal matter—and thus less threatening to other states in the region. In this political-military environ-

---

[40] Krastev et al., 2010.

[41] Chivvis, 2009; James M. Goldgeier, *The Future of NATO,* New York: Council on Foreign Relations, 2010.

[42] Evan S. Medeiros, Keith Crane, Eric Heginbotham, Norman D. Levin, Julia F. Lowell, Angel Rabasa, and Somi Song, *Pacific Currents: The Responses of U.S. Allies and Security Partners in East Asia to China's Rise,* Santa Monica, Calif.: RAND Corporation, MG-736-AF, 2008.

ment, a U.S. decision to unilaterally withdraw from the INF Treaty or cooperatively dissolve the treaty with Russia could be viewed as destabilizing and create real challenges for America's allies in the region. While many states employ hedging strategies—engaging in trade relations with China while also preparing for a potentially more assertive rising power in the future—the end of the treaty and the potential deployment of regional missile forces would be an unwelcome development with the potential for dramatic domestic political repercussions.[43] Even considering a significant deterioration of U.S.-China relations or an aggressive turn in Chinese foreign policy that alarms its neighbors and drives leaders to take actions to deter future PRC transgressions, medium-range missiles may not be viewed as an attractive capability. In short, it is a highly dubious assumption that U.S. missiles would be welcome in East Asian states, even if China's behavior increased threat perceptions over time.

Theater Missiles in East Asia

It is difficult to envision a scenario in which the United States withdraws from the INF Treaty and announces plans to develop and deploy land-based intermediate-range conventional ballistic missiles for use in East Asia that is not perceived by China as highly threatening.[44] Given the deep levels of trade and financial interdependence among regional actors, the potential costs of a diplomatic crisis will be viewed as unacceptably high. While Japan and South Korea may view Chinese long-term intentions with suspicion, the U.S. decision to withdraw from the INF Treaty to expressly rectify a perceived military imbalance with China likely would increase tensions between Beijing and Washington, placing leaders in Tokyo and Seoul in tenuous positions. Rather than dampening a potential conflict and contributing to regional stability, the U.S. move would likely be viewed as provocative and destabilizing. The ultimate intensity of the reaction will be determined by the state of the bilateral relations between China and its neighbors at the time. As

---

[43] Evan S. Medeiros, "Strategic Hedging and the Future of Asia-Pacific Stability," *Washington Quarterly*, Vol. 29, No. 1, 2005.

[44] Interviews conducted by the author, Washington, DC, April–May 2010.

allies who cooperate closely with U.S. forces in the region, both South Korea and Japan play important roles in the ability of the United States to project power and respond to crises. But neither seeks a direct confrontation with China, nor do they seek to see the United States introduce a new, potentially volatile rivalry to the region.[45]

Moreover, while the Chinese missile buildup has placed U.S. forward bases such as Kadena and Kunsan at risk, it is highly unlikely that either country would seek or accept new U.S. INF missiles on their territory, limiting an initial U.S. deployment to Guam or other holdings in Micronesia. While South Korea hosts significant U.S. military capabilities, these are clearly dedicated to the deterrence and defense against a North Korean threat, and Seoul does not view China in the same way that Washington does.[46] Intermediate-range missiles could only be viewed as being targeted at China, and there is little indication that Seoul would be willing to damage its positive relations with China to improve the United States capacity to defend Taiwan.[47] Similarly, the deployment of INF in Japan would be equally provocative and viewed as exclusively focused on China. Despite increasing concerns about China's future intentions, the agreement to host offensive missiles would place Tokyo clearly in an anti-Chinese coalition, and potentially would signal a dramatic shift in Japan's foreign and security policy.[48] Domestic political responses are likely to be vehemently opposed to such a deployment, barring a major shift in Chinese policy. Asking allies to take on a much more offensive role in hosting theater missiles—and thus asking them to become a direct target of Chinese missiles—is unlikely to be well-received, as the European experience of the early 1980s reflects.

---

[45] T. J. Pempel, "Japan's Search for the 'Sweet Spot': International Cooperation and Regional Security in Northeast Asia," *Orbis,* Vol. 55, No. 2, 2011; Richard J. Samuels, "Japan's Goldilock's Strategy," *Washington Quarterly,* Vol. 29, No. 4, 2006.

[46] Medeiros et al., 2008, pp. 72–73.

[47] Sunhyuk Kim and Wonhyuk Lim, "How to Deal with South Korea," *Washington Quarterly,* Vol. 30, No. 2, 2007.

[48] Christopher W. Hughes, *Japan's Remilitarization,* London: International Institute for Strategic Studies, 2009.

Over time, if China indeed embraced a more assertive and clearly threatening foreign policy, further options may open for the United States to deploy intermediate-range missile forces in the region, but domestic political reactions may continue to preclude such deployments.[49] Even with a more aggressive China, however, it may be difficult to obtain Japanese consent for a deployment precisely because it would make the home islands a priority target for Chinese forces. While U.S. forward bases already may be targets for a well-coordinated missile strike in the event of a Taiwan conflict, it can be argued that the deployment of missile forces targeted on China would be qualitatively more provocative to Beijing, and thus increase the probability of being attacked in the event of a conflict.

Russian Missiles in the East

While planners may be focused on the perceived need to respond to the gap created by Chinese missiles, a U.S. withdrawal or cooperative dissolution of the INF Treaty obviously would allow Russia to develop and deploy medium- and intermediate-range missiles on its territory. This could allow Russia to effectively increase its profile as a Pacific power in a fairly inexpensive way. The deployment of Russian missiles would certainly provide China with a new set of concerns that may complicate Chinese planning. However, Russian missiles will not simply be serving U.S. strategic objectives. These forces may also have a highly destabilizing impact on the East Asian region. For example, Japan is likely to view this development as highly threatening. Russia and Japan recently have engaged in an acrimonious diplomatic dispute over the Kurile Islands, and Russia has targeted Japan as a potential future adversary.[50] The prospect of Russian INF forces, particularly nuclear-armed missiles, dramatically alters Japan's security environment and would necessitate a response from its ally. This scenario should give

---

[49] Tsuyoshi Sunohara, "The Anatomy of Japan's Shifting Security Orientation," *Washington Quarterly*, Vol. 33, No. 4, 2010.

[50] Fred Weir, "Russia's Renewed Focus on Kuril Islands Draws Japanese Ire," *Christian Science Monitor*, February 11, 2011.

policymakers significant pause about the longer-term implications of a withdrawal from the INF Treaty.

Nonproliferation and Other Regional Trends

It is difficult to predict the nature of proliferation trends after a U.S. withdrawal from the INF Treaty. However, a few points seem fairly clear. First, the U.S. withdrawal is likely to seriously undermine the MTCR. Members of the regime are not bound from developing and producing their own missile systems. But given the critical role the United States and its close allies have played in the development and expansion of the regime, a unilateral U.S. withdrawal would seem to reverse a 20-year commitment to nonproliferation that has made substantial progress. Washington's unilateral rejection of negotiated restraints of a treaty that it created, and ostensible entrance into the development of intermediate-range missiles, seemingly would be incompatible with the goals of the MTCR. While many of the advanced industrial states are likely to maintain their export controls and continue to follow the MTCR, we may expect that other states, perhaps in the developing world, may take a different approach. At the very least, withdrawal from the INF would be a symbolic blow to U.S. leadership on the issue of preventing the spread of ballistic and cruise missile technologies.[51] Washington already struggles with a perception problem in its cooperation with Israel or India—two states outside the regime—on ballistic missile defenses. MTCR member states have expressed concerns that this is a *de facto* (if not *de jure*) double standard that inherently undermines the credibility of the regime.[52] The United States would open itself to claims of a double standard that have been so prevalent in debates over the Nonproliferation Regime.[53] Finally, the Proliferation Security Initiative, which is highly dependent on U.S. leadership and

---

[51] Joshua Pollack, "Missile Control: A Multi-Decade Experiment in Nonproliferation," *Bulletin of the Atomic Scientists*, August 1, 2011.

[52] Sidhu, 2007.

[53] Feickert, 2003, p. 10.

already faces problems due to its relatively ad hoc and informal character, would face increased difficulties moving forward.[54] Allies that view the U.S. withdrawal from the INF Treaty as complicating their regional security objectives may become less willing to engage in PSI-related activities if they threaten to directly challenge a regional competitor or make their diplomatic relations more difficult.[55] While it is unclear as to whether perceptions of hypocrisy create real costs for U.S. policy, given the seeming successes of nonproliferation efforts over the past two decades, the potential for undermining those efforts should be assessed.[56]

Perhaps more importantly, two states that have had previously questionable records in the proliferation arena—Russia and China—may have fewer concerns about maintaining robust export controls on missile technologies, and therefore engage in further proliferation. While it may be possible to work with Russia in the dissolution of the INF Treaty to create safeguards or accepted rules for the proliferation of missile components to third parties, it seems unlikely that China, being the primary target of new U.S. missile programs, would continue to abide by nonproliferation protocols. While China's early behavior in the nonproliferation realm was not exemplary, it has attempted to improve its export control and adhere to MTCR rules over much of the past decade. With the U.S. withdrawal from INF, it would not be surprising for China to engage in *strategic* proliferation, if for no other reason than expanded missile capabilities in a variety of states would further hamper U.S. missile defense capabilities, something that is particularly threatening to China. The proliferation of missile technologies to states that the United States views as problems, such as Myanmar, would be a relatively easy and inexpensive way to reciprocate against a U.S. policy constructed to "contain" China. Moreover, withholding support or blocking U.S.-initiated multilateral attempts to limit Iranian or North Korean missile programs would raise the costs of and

---

[54] Boese, 2008.

[55] Valencia, 2007.

[56] Antonia Chayes, "How American Treaty Behavior Threatens National Security," *International Security*, Vol. 33, No. 1, 2008.

limit the effectiveness of U.S. policies. Similarly, given its long history of missile development, it would seem likely that Russia would take advantage of the freedom to develop new intermediate-range systems to enhance its economic position by selling programs and technologies to states around the world, particularly if Moscow faced an economic downturn. Both states may have continuing security interests in nonproliferation, but with the United States withdrawal, both would face strategic and economic incentives to transfer missile systems and related technologies to other states and compromise their respective commitments to adhere to the MTCR.

Similarly, second-tier proliferators currently outside the MTCR may have less compunction about exporting sensitive missile-related systems if the perceived role of the United States in leading and supporting global nonproliferation initiatives is significantly weakened.[57] The United States and its allies have committed significant effort and resources to limiting the capacity of states like North Korea, Iran, and Syria to engage in proliferation activities. But these states and others such as India, Pakistan, and Israel may face greater incentives to export missile technologies in a more permissive nonproliferation environment.[58]

More generally, it is difficult to predict potential trends in horizontal proliferation. For example, in South America, both Argentina (1993) and Brazil (1995) are signatories to the MTCR.[59] Given their long-standing joint leadership of the cooperative economic organization MERCOSUR, and more recently the more politically focused Union of South American Nations, these two large states are in a favorable position to work toward a missile-free zone on the continent. These countries both possess the technical and industrial capabilities to develop intermediate-range missiles but have chosen to forego them. The increasing institutionalization of South American politics provides a new venue for the partner nations to explore the issue in the con-

---

[57] Feickert, 2003, p. 11.

[58] Sidhu, 2007.

[59] Feickert, 2003, p. 9; Mistry, 2003, pp. 74–88.

text of the South American Defense Council.[60] For example, while Venezuela persists in charting its own anti-U.S. course under Hugo Chavez, it has engaged in many of these regional organizations. It may be optimistic to predict that Venezuela would join in a "missile-free zone" agreement, but the diplomatic building blocks for a strong nonproliferation framework exist in South America. Attempts to acquire or to develop the capabilities to produce even short-range ballistic missiles are likely to be met with alarm, condemnation, and very likely isolation. Moreover, United States insistence that the possession of such weapons will not be allowed in the Western Hemisphere will play a critical deterrent role in reinforcing the emerging norms of the region. Given the relatively benign security environment and growing trends toward economic and political integration in South America, it seems unlikely that the abrogation of the INF Treaty by the United States and Russia would spur efforts to acquire intermediate-range missile forces. Nonetheless, insofar as general nonproliferation trends are likely to be undermined by an end to the Treaty and some measure of U.S. leadership will be questioned, it may be more difficult for a nation like Venezuela to be isolated in the longer-term or for a rising state such as Brazil or Argentina to forgo such capabilities.

Unilateral or Cooperative: Does the Nature of Withdrawal Make a Difference?

Even with a highly sensitive, comprehensive diplomatic strategy for laying the necessary groundwork for mitigating negative reactions, it is difficult to envision a scenario in which the unilateral U.S. withdrawal from the INF Treaty would provide military benefits in addressing the challenge of Chinese military modernization that would outweigh the significant and far-reaching political and security costs of doing so. Moreover, the decision to cooperatively dissolve the Treaty through a

---

[60] Alex Sanchez, "The South American Defense Council, UNASUR, the Latin American Military and the Region's Political Process," Council on Hemispheric Affairs, October 1, 2008.

negotiation process with Russia is unlikely to effectively mitigate those potential costs. Close consultations with NATO, Japan, South Korea, and other regional allies and partners would seem to be a central requisite of any U.S. diplomatic approach. A clear and significant deterioration in relations with China also would seem to be a necessary condition for any move in this direction. Nonetheless, precisely because of the potential negative implications of a world without the INF Treaty for the security of so many states, it will be exceedingly difficult for Washington to develop measures that can effectively reassure allies that, despite its willingness to alter the preferred status quo, the United States remains committed to supporting their security concerns. For example, further commitments to expand regional ballistic missile defense systems are likely to prove both hollow and ineffectual, due to the potentially greater missile forces that any such systems would need to address. Similarly, as discussed above, U.S. commitments to deploy its own conventional land-based theater missile systems to vulnerable states are only likely to precipitate significant domestic political resistance within those states. The end of the INF Treaty, regardless of the way it occurs, will have significant security costs for the United States and others.

Conventional INF or Geographic Limits: Could the Treaty be Revised?

One Russian commentator, writing in 2007 in the wake of President Putin's public threat to withdrawal from the INF Treaty, offered the potential solution of fundamentally revising the document. A revised INF Treaty would maintain existing prohibitions on nuclear-armed intermediate-range missile systems, but alter the Treaty's obligations to allow the United States and Russia to build conventional theater missile systems.[61] This approach would provide a remedy to what both states perceive as the growing challenges presented by regional powers with

---

[61] "Russian Pundit Suggest INF Treaty Change to Allow Non-Nuclear-Capable Missiles," *BBC Worldwide Monitoring*, March 2, 2007.

expanding missile forces. As the history of the negotiation of the INF Treaty reflects, verification and compliance issues seriously undermine the efficacy of such an initiative.[62] The INF Treaty contained provisions for extensive monitoring, including intrusive on-sight inspection. Ultimately, the decision to effectively ban all nuclear and conventional ballistic and cruise missiles of 500 to 5,500 km, as well as their development, production, and testing, was premised on the shared agreement that the nature of the weapon made any lesser constraints susceptible to cheating. Given the long-standing ability of both states to develop nuclear and non-nuclear missile programs, an agreement that prohibited only nuclear-armed missiles would prove almost impossible to verify. While the United States and Russia may no longer be adversaries, they are also not friends.[63] As the negotiations over the "New START" Treaty reflected, concerns were expressed on both sides about verification and explicit counting rules and guidelines as a corrective to the less rigorous 2003 Moscow Treaty.[64] Moreover, the latent capability to place nuclear warheads on ostensibly conventionally armed (but likely dual-use) missile systems would create a virtual nuclear capability with potentially destabilizing dynamics for regional security. Just as the current Chinese missile program presents a longer-term threat of dramatically increasing the number of nuclear armed systems that Beijing can deploy, a "conventional-only" treaty would do little do assuage the fears of future expansions and complicate existing arms control agreements between the United States and Russia. In short, such an agreement is likely to cause more problems than it solves, which is why it does not seem to constitute a realistic choice for the United States or Russia.

Similarly, any agreement that sought to limit the deployment of new INF missiles (whether conventional or nuclear) to certain geographic locations would only reopen verification problems that proved difficult to address without "global" limitation during the negotiation of the original Treaty. For example, having allowed the Soviet Union

---

[62] Rueckert, 1993, p. 80.

[63] Arbatov, 2011, p. 34.

[64] Ibid.

to maintain a certain number of SS-20s east of the Ural Mountains would have perpetuated the threat that these weapons could be moved back into positions that could threaten Western Europe in the future. Moreover, such a solution would have only exacerbated tensions in East Asia and presented U.S. allies such as Japan with a direct and persistent threat to their security. The idea of limiting deployments of new INF missiles to the home territory of the two signatory states would fundamentally favor Russia, given its geographic position as a European, Central, and East Asian power.[65] Such an agreement clearly would do little to address the perceived problems of extended deterrence in East Asia that have driven U.S. experts to consider the need for such systems if they were limited to deployment within the continental United States. While Guam is a U.S. territory, it is unclear that Russia would view deployments there as legitimate. As the negotiations of the INF Treaty reflect, measures short of a complete prohibition against land-based theater missiles would create significant problems of verification and compliance. As a result, any revisions based on either warhead types or geographic limitations are likely to decrease security and erode stability in critical regions, thus undermining, rather than supporting, U.S. security interests.

---

[65] Nikolai Khorunzhiy, "Should Russia Quit the Treaty on Medium- and Short-Range Missiles?" *RIA Novosti*, April 11, 2007.

CHAPTER SIX

Potential Ways Forward for the United States and the Future of the INF Treaty

Having examined the expected military benefits of conventional intermediate-range ballistic missile forces for U.S. forces in East Asia in addressing the growing threat of Chinese missiles, as well as the larger potential political and security implications of withdrawing from the INF Treaty, this chapter discusses potential ways forward for U.S. policymakers. Ultimately, two broad policy choices seem to emerge from the analysis up to this point: the maintenance of the status quo, in which the United States and Russia remain bound by the INF Treaty while others are free to acquire and develop such systems, and the pursuit of a comprehensive agreement based on the 2007 Russian proposal to expand or "multilateralize" the treaty. Each of these policies will be explored in detail and assessed in terms of their implications for U.S. security. To provide context for an analysis of these potential approaches, this chapter will briefly discuss the prevailing trends in Russian and Chinese views on arms control.

Russian and Chinese Views on Arms Control

Russia and the United States share a long history of strategic arms control negotiations. Aside from providing Russia with a prestige that no other state can claim, arms control negotiations are a means through which Russia can maintain its nuclear deterrent and reinforce strategic stability by restraining U.S. strategic programs.[1] Nonetheless, throughout the most recent New START process, it became increasingly clear that the agreed-upon numerical levels for strategic systems were actually above what Russia would be capable of fielding. So while the United States actually would make cuts under the new Treaty, mostly through retirement of systems, Russia would be unlikely to achieve the levels without a significant buildup.[2] Due to retirements of obsolete programs and difficulties in developing and producing new replacement systems, Russia's strategic arsenal may fall to 350 to 400 delivery vehicles and 1,000 to 1,100 warheads under New START's counting rules, well below the allowed 700 delivery vehicle/1,550 warhead ceiling set out in the Treaty. Within Russian policy circles, there has been significant debate about how best to rectify this potential gap in capabilities, with the development of a new "heavy" ICBM capable of carrying ten Multiple Independently Targeted Reentry Vehicles MIRVs as a potential solution.[3] Such a development would seem to reverse the momentum toward strategic level reductions signified by New START but also reflects some Russian elites' sense of strategic vulnerability. This perceived weakness is not simply a product of the quantitative decline in the Russian strategic arsenal, but also a clear indication of the impact of the planned expansion of U.S. BMD and the development of conventional strategic weapons on Russian thinking.[4] Russia could also, logically, seek for a follow-on agreement to START that further reduces the arsenals, but the acrimony and division exhibited in the ratification processes in both Moscow and Washington make further strategic cuts seems unlikely. Considering the expressed priorities of both Putin and Medvedev to invest in the modernization of Russia's conventional mili-

---

[1] Oliker et al., 2009, p. 170; Nikolai Sokov, "The Evolving Role of Nuclear Weapons in Russia's Security Policy," in *Engaging China and Russia on Nuclear Disarmament*, eds. Cristina Hansell and William C. Potter, Monterey: James Martin Center for Nonproliferation Studies, 2009, pp. 73–76.

[2] Tom Z. Collina, "Russia Below Some New START Limits," *Arms Control Today*, July/August 2011.

[3] Arbatov, 2011, p. 15.

[4] Ibid., pp. 17–18; Oliker et al., 2009, p. 170.

tary forces, further strategic nuclear reductions would free up resources that could be channeled into conventional programs. However, without some acceptable resolution on U.S. ballistic missile defenses, conventional prompt global strike, non-strategic (or tactical) nuclear weapons in Europe, and adjustments to Conventional Forces Europe Treaty, Moscow is unlikely to engage in further negotiations.[5] These issues are likely to make it difficult to cooperate closely on the issue of expanding INF, but clearly reflect the importance of engaging Moscow in a more comprehensive way on security and arms control issues.

China's views of arms control vis-à-vis the United States is quite different from that of Russia. Having taken a very different path in the development of its strategic nuclear deterrent force from the two superpowers, Beijing considers discussions of limitations or reductions on strategic systems as having limited relevance to its situation. With a small arsenal of delivery vehicles and a relatively small number of warheads, China seemingly has embraced the view that deterrence is relatively easy to achieve with a capacity for "assured retaliation" or perhaps the "minimal means of reprisal."[6] In fact, before Beijing considers limitations on its programs, it argues that it is incumbent on Washington and Moscow to greatly reduce their forces.[7] Chinese leaders perceive arms control as a means with which the United States can maintain its "absolute security" and "hegemony" within the existing system, while also attempting to occupy the moral high ground without actually sacrificing its own capabilities.[8] Reductions in nuclear weapons have less meaning when expansion of ABM defense and conventional strategic systems are under development.

Thus, while the rhetoric of the Obama administration in support of a world without nuclear weapons was generally welcomed in Chinese policy circles, the subsequent NPR failed to live up to the

---

[5] Arbatov, 2011, pp. 20–23.

[6] Fravel and Medeiros, 2010; Lewis, 2007.

[7] Saalman, 2009, pp. 52–53.

[8] Saalman, 2011, p. 15.

lofty expectations.[9] Moreover, in China's view, the 2010 NPR failed to "replace" the controversial 2001 NPR which was viewed as potentially lowering the threshold for using nuclear weapons and/or developing conventional strategic weapons that could indeed be utilized without the difficulties of breaking the nuclear taboo.[10] Chinese elites continue to view the United States as attempting to maximize its freedom with regard to the capabilities it deploys to maintain its security. Though those elites see that is willing to lead on global arms control issues, it also hedges against potential threat.[11]

A difficult challenge in negotiating any arms control agreement with China is its fundamentally different view on stability and transparency.[12] Given the quantitative imbalance between the two states' nuclear arsenals, China is extremely reticent to engage in Cold War-type negotiations in which numbers of warheads and delivery vehicles would be shared. Ambiguity and secrecy are viewed as playing an important role in maintaining its nuclear deterrent with relatively small numbers of warheads and delivery vehicles, though the latter are expanding significantly.[13] For China, this strategic stability—like that achieved after nuclear parity during the later Cold War—really doesn't apply to the relationship between the United States and China. Larger U.S. and Russian reductions to strategic forces are seen as necessary before China should consider discussion limitations on its strategic forces.[14]

However, this does not mean that China would be unwilling to engage in negotiations. The prestige attached would certainly rein-

---

[9] Ibid., pp. 13–14.

[10] Ibid., pp. 22–26.

[11] Ibid.

[12] Ibid., p. 18.

[13] Jeffrey Lewis, "Chinese Nuclear Posture and Force Modernization," in *Engaging China and Russia on Nuclear Disarmament*, eds. Cristina Hansell and William C. Potter, Monterey: James Martin Center for Nonproliferation Studies, 2009, p. 37.

[14] Saalman, 2011, pp. 4–9.

force the image of China as a rising global power.[15] At the same time, China has been willing to play a constructive role in the Conference on Disarmament, and it signed the Comprehensive Test Ban Treaty.[16] Conversely, it has obstructed negotiations on the fissile material cutoff treaty (FMCT), which some have interpreted as Beijing reserving its right to acquire additional stocks of fissile material in response to a changing security environment and a threat to its existing arsenal.[17]

Clearly, both Russia and China share two major concerns: the expansion of U.S. BMD capabilities and the perceived interest in the United States to develop conventional strategic weapons, most notably PGS. While land-based intermediate-range ballistic and cruise missiles are not directly linked to these programs, these systems could provide China and Russia with a convenient countermeasure to theater ballistic missile defenses, particularly in key regions. As discussed previously, a world with fewer missiles only increases the expected effectiveness of proposed missile defenses.[18] A discussion of U.S. missile defenses, particularly in regional security contexts, would likely need to be a component of (or the central discussion topic of concurrent to) any negotiations on the expansion of the INF Treaty. Moreover, given Russia's concerns about U.S. and NATO BMD in Central Europe, it would seem that some understanding between the two on BMD would be necessary to obtain Russian cooperation in approaching China. Conventional PGS may be a subject that could be addressed in a different venue, perhaps on future strategic reductions.

---

[15] Cristina Hansell and Nikita Perfilyev, "Strategic Relations between the United States, Russia, and China and the Possibility of Cooperation on Disarmament," in *Engaging China and Russia on Nuclear Disarmament*, eds. Cristina Hansell and William C. Potter, Monterey: James Martin Center for Nonproliferation Studies, 2009, pp. 138–39.

[16] Lewis, 2007, pp. 21-22.

[17] Lewis, 2009.

[18] Richard Speier, "Missile Nonproliferation and Missile Defense: Fiting Them Together," *Arms Control Today*, November 2007.

Maintaining the Status Quo

In the short term, given the difficulties of coordinating joint policies of expanding the INF Treaty with Russia, and the low probability of Chinese receptiveness to engage in negotiations, the maintenance of the status quo would seem a prudent policy for the United States. Because of the high political and security costs associated with abrogation of the INF Treaty discussed in the previous chapter, and the limited expected military benefits of theater missiles for U.S. capabilities in the addressing the threat of China's missile expansion, working to keep Russia engaged in the Treaty regime seems to support U.S. interests. The INF Treaty clearly has contributed to the security and stability of regions critical to U.S. national interests, most importantly Europe, and thus provides clear, if often taken for granted, benefits for the United States. Withdrawing from the Treaty and freeing Russia to develop new land-based intermediate-range missiles not only will significantly alter the European security environment, but could complicate the East Asian region as well, as Japan may be confronted with a Russian INF threat.

Moreover, while incomplete, the MTCR has significantly restrained the progress of horizontal proliferation since the 1990s, and the ICOC has attempted to instantiate norms of nonproliferation. Minimizing the proliferation of missile programs and the flow of missile technologies would seem to support U.S. security interests, and the MTCR, with further cooperative measures such as the Proliferation Security Initiative, provides a solid foundation for combating proliferation in the future. The perpetuation of the INF Treaty reinforces global trends that have limited the number of states with intermediate-range missile capabilities to those discussed in this study. Given U.S. investments in regional and global missile defense systems, a world with fewer rather than more missiles greatly enhances the probability that these systems will make a contribution to the security of the United States and their allies in the future. Beyond the significant and far-reaching political and security costs of a withdrawal from the Treaty, the presence of new and active suppliers like Russia and China will greatly erode the potential value of any U.S. missile defense investments and exacerbate the challenge confronting the United States.

In addition, as discussed in Chapter 4, the threat created by the expansion of Chinese missile forces can be addressed with other military and diplomatic measures in both the shorter and longer terms. Concerns for the U.S. deterrent can be addressed in several ways. Investments in maintaining or, if necessary, expanding stocks of air- and sea-launched cruise missiles, which can be delivered by existing platforms such as the SSGN and standoff bombers such as the B-1, will enhance any perceived gap in U.S. capabilities in the shorter term. In the medium term, revisiting concepts such as the Navy's "Arsenal Ship" may be a relatively cost-effective means to significantly enhance the offensive capabilities available to combatant commanders in the Western Pacific. An "Arsenal Airplane" based on civilian jetliners such as the Boeing 737 could fill a gap in U.S. standoff bomber capabilities, but the costs may make the platform less attractive. In the longer term, investments in a next-generation family of bombers, both penetrating and standoff, will provide a formidable and versatile capability for enhancing the U.S. deterrent during crisis or executing missions should deterrence fail. Similarly, new air- and sea-launched cruise missile systems and precision guided munitions that maximize the capabilities of these platforms against advanced air and missile defenses would be prudent areas to focus investment.

The United States also may enhance its capacity to deny Chinese objectives in a potential conflict by decreasing the probability of success in an anti-access/area denial campaign against U.S. forward bases in the region. Improvement in active defenses, including ballistic missile defenses, and passive defenses, including the hardening of bases and improving the capacity of the United States to recover from attack through the deployment of runway replacement kits, can increase the risk facing Chinese planners and sustain the ability of the United States to respond to a conflict. Over the longer term, diversification of bases in the region and the consistent hardening of C4ISR capabilities in the region to undermine the potential gains of a coordinated first strike could decrease the expected benefits of such an attack. Given the geography of the Western Pacific, and considering Beijing's commitment of resources to develop and deploy expansive intermediate-range missile capabilities, it is unclear that U.S. actions can entirely check China's efforts. However, the prescriptions offered here can offset them in ways that maintain robust deterrent and denial capabilities in the event of a crisis without assuming the political and security costs of withdrawing from the INF Treaty.

As the analysis of this study has made clear, it is difficult to envision a scenario in which the military benefits of a new land-based, intermediate-range ballistic missile would approach the far-reaching and significant political and security costs associated with a withdrawal from the INF Treaty. At the same time, the continuing expansion of Chinese intermediate-range missiles and the potential for a large number of them to be equipped with nuclear weapons presents a longer-term challenge. With a nuclear INF force, China may seek to coerce and intimidate regional allies, undermining U.S. interests and objectives and potentially creating pressures for the United States to respond.[19] Moreover, pressures on Russia may also increase as its strategic arsenal declines and China's nuclear INF forces expand. Consequently, the United States should seek to expand the INF, following Russia's 2007 proposal. This likely will be a difficult process, but if the United States could engage Russia, China, and other relevant states in a process that succeeded in eliminating these weapons, it would significantly improve the security of regions vital to U.S. interests.

Expanding the INF Treaty

Acknowledging Russia's security concerns arising from missile programs that the INF Treaty proscribes, and accepting the diplomatic and security benefits provided by the Treaty, the United States should work closely with Russia to expand its membership to other regional powers, most notably China. In order to effectively "pressure" Beijing to engage in negotiation with the implicit or explicit threat of abrogat-

---

[19]   Mark Stokes and Dan Blumenthal, "Can a Treaty Contain China's Missiles?" *Washington Post*, January 2, 2011.

ing the Treaty, the United States and Russia seemingly would have to resolve or set aside several outstanding security issues, including U.S. plans for ballistic missile defense, conventional military disparities, and the role of non-strategic nuclear weapons in Europe. More specifically, the revision of the Conventional Forces in Europe Treaty (CFE) has emerged as a major impediment to deepening relations between the United States and Russia and improving relations between Russia and Europe.[20] While the former superpower rivals are no longer adversaries, there remains significant mistrust, particularly over longer-term goals and objectives. Reiterating strong support for the Russian proposal to globalize the INF Treaty in the Committee on Disarmament would be a first step toward broaching the idea of a partnership on the issue. But important issues, many of which require some measure of reassuring Russia about U.S. intentions, likely will be a requisite to truly meaningful cooperation.

Expanding the INF Treaty will be a difficult task, given the importance that intermediate-range ballistic and cruise missiles have assumed in the arsenals of important states such as China, India, and Pakistan, and the relationships among them. However, the combined diplomatic leverage of the United States and Russia could prove effective in engaging other states in a security dialogue that addresses underlying threats and the perceived needs for these theater-missile forces. Initial overtures to China would seem a prudent first step, and while the modernization of China's missile forces are a clear priority for Beijing (and one that would not be restrained without significant concessions), a trilateral security dialogue could prove useful in building confidence and decreasing uncertainty over time. Moreover, the focus on intermediate-range ballistic and cruise missiles—a tangible capability with significant military and political influence—may allow the three states to discuss issues without being diverted to more abstract discussions of "strategic stability" or deeper nuclear reductions.[21]

---

[20] F. Stephen Larrabee and David E. Mosher, "Rebuilding Arms Control," *United Press International,* August 10, 2007.

[21] Saalman, 2009, pp. 4–9.

Because of the disparities in capabilities of the United States and Russia vis-à-vis China, broader approaches to arms control or reductions are unlikely to succeed. However, at present rates of deployment, it will be increasingly difficult for China to sustain the argument that its land-based, intermediate-range missiles, when equipped with nuclear warheads, are not appropriate for discussion, given the potential threat they pose to Russia and to U.S. allies in East Asia. The United States and Russia may initially have viewed these systems as *theater* missiles, but given the geography of East, Central, and South Asia, they are effectively *strategic* weapons. Over time, India and Pakistan, both of whom possess land-based IRBMs capable of striking China and Russia and thus figure into Beijing's and Moscow's strategic calculations, could be invited into the strategic dialogue, providing the rivals with a venue to further build confidence and address the strategic aspects of their ongoing conflict.

A second, complimentary track to such an approach would be to engage current MTCR member states in joining the multilateral INF Treaty to further isolate and pressure those states with significant INF programs and restrict their ability to expand on existing arsenals. MTCR member states are generally those capable of building and exporting missiles and missile-related technologies, and so they would be effectively asked to forego the development of INF missiles in the future. The MTRC members could further promulgate guidelines to significantly constrain access to technologies related to advanced land-based intermediate-range cruise missiles. This could be bolstered by subsequent revisions of the ICOC to directly address cruise missiles in its guidelines and by offering its membership the ability to join the INF Treaty.

A third approach, which could also compliment the first two, would be a regional one. The United States (ideally working with Russia) would attempt to enlist China's neighbors in the cause of pressuring Beijing to explain its continued buildup of intermediate-range missiles despite the warming of relations with Taiwan. The sheer quantity of intermediate-range delivery vehicles that Beijing has accumulated seems inordinate to the task of deterring Taiwan's independence. While China has pledged not to threaten non-nuclear states with nuclear weapons, the continued expansion of missile forces should be threatening to other East Asian states. These land-based IRBMs provide China with a conventional capability, as well as a formidable and growing nuclear capability, that could dramatically alter the nature of regional politics. The United States should work closely with Tokyo, Seoul, and perhaps other states in the region to engage China and express their concerns about the growing conventional threat to their security and the longer-term potential nuclear threat. Existing forums such as the Six-Party Talks or the ASEAN Regional Forum could be used to initiate these discussions and place pressure on China to explain its buildup of these systems and perhaps to take measures to reassure worried neighbors.

An alternative regional approach would be to engage various states in missile test bans. Whether in East Asia, the Subcontinent, or even the Middle East, working with states to cooperatively agree to ban testing on short- and medium-range missiles could provide a basis for further negotiations and, over time, an expansion of the INF Treaty. This regional approach may be more applicable to states and more appropriately place their missile programs in the context of underlying security challenges than a broader, global approach.[22]

One approach that would seem less effective would involve a U.S. threat to withdraw from the Treaty and to deploy a new generation of missiles to coerce Beijing to engage Washington and Moscow in negotiations on INF Treaty expansion. As the study has shown, the potential political and security costs of a U.S. withdrawal would make such a threat relatively incredible. Given the fiscal and budgetary constraints confronting the United States, the threat to build and deploy an expensive new program also seems improbable. In fact, China likely would view both such threats as a bluff, or if carried out, favorable to Chinese interests. The United States may undermine its own diplomatic positions while committing scarce resources to a program that may be less threatening to China than a long-range strike, conventional PGS, and BMD, and less effective for actually addressing China's missile threat, as Chapter 4 contends.

---

[22] Michael Elleman, "Containing Iran's Missile Threat," *Survival*, Vol. 54, No. 1, 2012.

Given the current differences in perceptions and overall approaches to strategic issues among the United States, Russia, and China, a dialogue that allowed for the development of some measure of common understanding concerning priorities and motives would provide the basis for a more credible attempt to push China, with Russian support, into examining the implications of its missile buildup and the potential reactions that the United States and Russia could take to respond. In fact, a U.S. threat to withdraw from the INF Treaty and develop and deploy new land-based IRBMs would seem far more credible in a context in which China understood the potential costs attached to a U.S. (and Russian) withdrawal and the commitment of the United States (and Russia) to address the perceived threat created by China's missiles.

This is not to assume that it would be easy to obtain the type of deep cooperation with Russia required to achieve the perception of joint leverage in negotiations with Beijing. Nor should we expect that China would simply forego a capability that has become the centerpiece of its capacity to avert the loss of Taiwan in the event of a conflict. However, engaging Russia, China, and others in a larger dialogue to expand the INF Treaty would be a relatively costless means to acquire important information and signal a willingness to cooperatively address common challenges in the security realm. It may be a long and painstaking process to achieve any diplomatic success, but in the interim, the United States possesses effective means to protect its forward-deployed troops and key regional allies, and the perpetuation of the INF Treaty will continue to serves its national security interests.

The Intermediate-Range Nuclear Forces (INF) Treaty[1]

Treaty Between The United States Of America And The Union Of Soviet Socialist Republics On The Elimination Of Their Intermediate-Range And Shorter-Range Missiles

Signed at Washington December 8, 1987
Ratification advised by U.S. Senate May 27, 1988
Instruments of ratification exchanged June 1, 1988
Entered into force June 1, 1988
Proclaimed by U.S. President December 27, 1988

The United States of America and the Union of Soviet Socialist Republics, hereinafter referred to as the Parties,

Conscious that nuclear war would have devastating consequences for all mankind,

Guided by the objective of strengthening strategic stability,

Convinced that the measures set forth in this Treaty will help to reduce the risk of outbreak of war and strengthen international peace and security, and

---

[1] U.S. State Department, "Treaty Between The United States Of America And The Union Of Soviet Socialist Republics On The Elimination Of Their Intermediate-Range And Shorter-Range Missiles (INF Treaty)," Washington, D.C., December 8, 1987, online at http://www.state.gov/t/avc/trty/102360.htm as of May 15, 2012.

Mindful of their obligations under Article VI of the Treaty on the Non-Proliferation of Nuclear Weapons,

Have agreed as follows:

Article I

In accordance with the provisions of this Treaty which includes the Memorandum of Understanding and Protocols which form an integral part thereof, each Party shall eliminate its intermediate-range and shorter-range missiles, not have such systems thereafter, and carry out the other obligations set forth in this Treaty.

Article II

For the purposes of this Treaty:

1. The term "ballistic missile" means a missile that has a ballistic trajectory over most of its flight path. The term "ground-launched ballistic missile (GLBM)" means a ground-launched ballistic missile that is a weapon-delivery vehicle.

2. The term "cruise missile" means an unmanned, self-propelled vehicle that sustains flight through the use of aerodynamic lift over most of its flight path. The term "ground-launched cruise missile (GLCM)" means a ground-launched cruise missile that is a weapon-delivery vehicle.

3. The term "GLBM launcher" means a fixed launcher or a mobile land-based transporter-erector-launcher mechanism for launching a GLBM.

4. The term "GLCM launcher" means a fixed launcher or a mobile land-based transporter-erector-launcher mechanism for launching a GLCM.

5. The term "intermediate-range missile" means a GLBM or a GLCM having a range capability in excess of 1000 kilometers but not in excess of 5500 kilometers.

6. The term "shorter-range missile" means a GLBM or a GLCM having a range capability equal to or in excess of 500 kilometers but not in excess of 1000 kilometers.

7. The term "deployment area" means a designated area within which intermediate-range missiles and launchers of such missiles may operate and within which one or more missile operating bases are located.

8. The term "missile operating base" means:

(a) in the case of intermediate-range missiles, a complex of facilities, located within a deployment area, at which intermediate-range missiles and launchers of such missiles normally operate, in which support structures associated with such missiles and launchers are also located and in which support equipment associated with such missiles and launchers is normally located; and

(b) in the case of shorter-range missiles, a complex of facilities, located any place, at which shorter-range missiles and launchers of such missiles normally operate and in which support equipment associated with such missiles and launchers is normally located.

9. The term "missile support facility," as regards intermediate-range or shorter-range missiles and launchers of such missiles, means a missile production facility or a launcher production facility, a missile repair facility or a launcher repair facility, a training facility, a missile storage facility or a launcher storage facility, a test range, or an elimination facility as those terms are defined in the Memorandum of Understanding.

10. The term "transit" means movement, notified in accordance with paragraph 5(f) of Article IX of this Treaty, of an intermediate-range missile or a launcher of such a missile between missile support facilities, between such a facility and a deployment area or between deployment areas, or of a shorter-range missile or a launcher of such a missile from a missile support facility or a missile operating base to an elimination facility.

11. The term "deployed missile" means an intermediate-range missile located within a deployment area or a shorter-range missile located at a missile operating base.

12. The term "non-deployed missile" means an intermediate-range missile located outside a deployment area or a shorter-range missile located outside a missile operating base.

13. The term "deployed launcher" means a launcher of an intermediate-range missile located within a deployment area or a launcher of a shorter-range missile located at a missile operating base.

14. The term "non-deployed launcher" means a launcher of an intermediate-range missile located outside a deployment area or a launcher of a shorter-range missile located outside a missile operating base.

15. The term "basing country" means a country other than the United States of America or the Union of Soviet Socialist Republics on whose territory intermediate-range or shorter-range missiles of the Parties, launchers of such missiles or support structures associated with such missiles and launchers were located at any time after November 1, 1987. Missiles or launchers in transit are not considered to be "located."

Article III

1. For the purposes of this Treaty, existing types of intermediate-range missiles are:

(a) for the United States of America, missiles of the types designated by the United States of America as the Pershing II and the BGM-109G, which are known to the Union of Soviet Socialist Republics by the same designations; and

(b) for the Union of Soviet Socialist Republics, missiles of the types designated by the Union of Soviet Socialist Republics as the RSD-10, the R-12 and the R-14, which are known to the United States of America as the SS-20, the SS-4 and the SS-5, respectively.

2. For the purposes of this Treaty, existing types of shorter-range missiles are:

(a) for the United States of America, missiles of the type designated by the United States of America as the Pershing IA, which is known to the Union of Soviet Socialist Republics by the same designation; and

(b) for the Union of Soviet Socialist Republics, missiles of the types designated by the Union of Soviet Socialist Republics as the OTR-22 and the OTR-23, which are known to the United States of America as the SS-12 and the SS-23, respectively.

Article IV

1. Each Party shall eliminate all its intermediate-range missiles and launchers of such missiles, and all support structures and support equipment of the categories listed in the Memorandum of Understanding associated with such missiles and launchers, so that no later than three years after entry into force of this Treaty and thereafter no such missiles, launchers, support structures or support equipment shall be possessed by either Party.

2. To implement paragraph 1 of this Article, upon entry into force of this Treaty, both Parties shall begin and continue throughout the duration of each phase, the reduction of all types of their deployed and non-deployed intermediate-range missiles and deployed and non-deployed launchers of such missiles and support structures and support equipment associated with such missiles and launchers in accordance with the provisions of this Treaty. These reductions shall be implemented in two phases so that:

(a) by the end of the first phase, that is, no later than 29 months after entry into force of this Treaty:

(i) the number of deployed launchers of intermediate-range missiles for each Party shall not exceed the number of launchers that are capable of carrying or containing at one time missiles considered by the Parties to carry 171 warheads;

(ii) the number of deployed intermediate-range missiles for each Party shall not exceed the number of such missiles considered by the Parties to carry 180 warheads;

(iii) the aggregate number of deployed and non-deployed launchers of intermediate-range missiles for each Party shall not exceed the number of launchers that are capable of carrying or containing at one time missiles considered by the Parties to carry 200 warheads;

(iv) the aggregate number of deployed and non-deployed intermediate-range missiles for each Party shall not exceed the number of such missiles considered by the Parties to carry 200 warheads; and

(v) the ratio of the aggregate number of deployed and non-deployed intermediate-range GLBMs of existing types for each Party to the aggregate number of deployed and non-deployed intermediate-range missiles of existing types possessed by that Party shall not exceed the ratio of such intermediate-range GLBMs to such intermediate-range missiles for that Party as of November 1, 1987, as set forth in the Memorandum of Understanding; and

(b) by the end of the second phase, that is, no later than three years after entry into force of this Treaty, all intermediate-range missiles of each Party, launchers of such missiles and all support structures and support equipment of the categories listed in the Memorandum of Understanding associated with such missiles and launchers, shall be eliminated.

Article V

1. Each Party shall eliminate all its shorter-range missiles and launchers of such missiles, and all support equipment of the categories listed in the Memorandum of Understanding associated with such missiles and launchers, so that no later than 18 months after entry into force of this Treaty and thereafter no such missiles, launchers or support equipment shall be possessed by either Party.

2. No later than 90 days after entry into force of this Treaty, each Party shall complete the removal of all its deployed shorter-range missiles and deployed and non-deployed launchers of such missiles to elimination facilities and shall retain them at those locations until they are eliminated in accordance with the procedures set forth in the Protocol on Elimination. No later than 12 months after entry into force of this Treaty, each Party shall complete the removal of all its non-deployed shorter-range missiles to elimination facilities and shall retain them at those locations until they are eliminated in accordance with the procedures set forth in the Protocol on Elimination.

3. Shorter-range missiles and launchers of such missiles shall not be located at the same elimination facility. Such facilities shall be separated by no less than 1000 kilometers.

Article VI

1. Upon entry into force of this Treaty and thereafter, neither Party shall:

(a) produce or flight-test any intermediate-range missiles or produce any stages of such missiles or any launchers of such missiles; or

(b) produce, flight-test or launch any shorter-range missiles or produce any stages of such missiles or any launchers of such missiles.

2. Notwithstanding paragraph 1 of this Article, each Party shall have the right to produce a type of GLBM not limited by this Treaty which uses a stage which is outwardly similar to, but not interchangeable with, a stage of an existing type of intermediate-range GLBM having more than one stage, providing that that Party does not produce any other stage which is outwardly similar to, but not interchangeable with, any other stage of an existing type of intermediate-range GLBM.

Article VII

For the purposes of this Treaty:

1. If a ballistic missile or a cruise missile has been flight-tested or deployed for weapon delivery, all missiles of that type shall be considered to be weapon-delivery vehicles.

2. If a GLBM or GLCM is an intermediate-range missile, all GLBMs or GLCMs of that type shall be considered to be intermediate-range missiles. If a GLBM or GLCM is a shorter-range missile, all GLBMs or GLCMs of that type shall be considered to be shorter-range missiles.

3. If a GLBM is of a type developed and tested solely to intercept and counter objects not located on the surface of the earth, it shall not be considered to be a missile to which the limitations of this Treaty apply.

4. The range capability of a GLBM not listed in Article III of this Treaty shall be considered to be the maximum range to which it has been tested. The range capability of a GLCM not listed in Article III of this Treaty shall be considered to be the maximum distance which can be covered by the missile in its standard design mode flying until fuel exhaustion, determined by projecting its flight path onto the earth's sphere from the point of launch to the point of impact. GLBMs or GLCMs that have a range capability equal to or in excess of 500 kilometers but not in excess of 1000 kilometers shall be considered to be shorter-range missiles. GLBMs or GLCMs that have a range capability in excess of 1000 kilometers but not in excess of 5500 kilometers shall be considered to be intermediate-range missiles.

5. The maximum number of warheads an existing type of intermediate-range missile or shorter-range missile carries shall be considered to be the number listed for missiles of that type in the Memorandum of Understanding.

6. Each GLBM or GLCM shall be considered to carry the maximum number of warheads listed for a GLBM or GLCM of the type in the Memorandum of Understanding.

7. If a launcher has been tested for launching a GLBM or a GLCM, all launchers of that type shall be considered to have been tested for launching GLBMs or GLCMs.

8. If a launcher has contained or launched a particular type of GLBM or GLCM, all launchers of that type shall be considered to be launchers of that type of GLBM or GLCM.

9. The number of missiles each launcher of an existing type of intermediate-range missile or shorter-range missile shall be considered to be capable of carrying or containing at one time is the number listed for launchers of missiles of that type in the Memorandum of Understanding.

10. Except in the case of elimination in accordance with the procedures set forth in the Protocol on Elimination, the following shall apply:

(a) for GLBMs which are stored or moved in separate stages, the longest stage of an intermediate-range or shorter-range GLBM shall be counted as a complete missile;

(b) for GLBMs which are not stored or moved in separate stages, a canister of the type used in the launch of an intermediate-range GLBM, unless a Party proves to the satisfaction of the other Party that it does not contain such a missile, or an assembled intermediate-range or shorter-range GLBM, shall be counted as a complete missile; and

(c) for GLCMs, the airframe of an intermediate-range or shorter-range GLCM shall be counted as a complete missile.

11. A ballistic missile which is not a missile to be used in a ground-based mode shall not be considered to be a GLBM if it is test-launched at a test site from a fixed land-based launcher which is used solely for test purposes and which is distinguishable from GLBM launchers. A cruise missile which is not a missile to be used in a ground-based mode shall not be considered to be a GLCM if it is test-launched at a test site from a fixed land-based launcher which is used solely for test purposes and which is distinguishable from GLCM launchers.

12. Each Party shall have the right to produce and use for booster systems, which might otherwise be considered to be intermediate-range or shorter-range missiles, only existing types of booster stages for such booster systems. Launches of such booster systems shall not be considered to be flight-testing of intermediate-range or shorter-range missiles provided that:

(a) stages used in such booster systems are different from stages used in those missiles listed as existing types of intermediate-range or shorter-range missiles in Article III of this Treaty;

(b) such booster systems are used only for research and development purposes to test objects other than the booster systems themselves;

(c) the aggregate number of launchers for such booster systems shall not exceed 35 for each Party at any one time; and

(d) the launchers for such booster systems are fixed, emplaced above ground and located only at research and development launch sites which are specified in the Memorandum of Understanding.

Research and development launch sites shall not be subject to inspection pursuant to Article XI of this Treaty.

Article VIII

1. All intermediate-range missiles and launchers of such missiles shall be located in deployment areas, at missile support facilities or shall be in transit. Intermediate-range missiles or launchers of such missiles shall not be located elsewhere.

2. Stages of intermediate-range missiles shall be located in deployment areas, at missile support facilities or moving between deployment areas, between missile support facilities or between missile support facilities and deployment areas.

3. Until their removal to elimination facilities as required by paragraph 2 of Article V of this Treaty, all shorter-range missiles and launchers of such missiles shall be located at missile operating bases, at missile support facilities or shall be in transit. Shorter-range missiles or launchers of such missiles shall not be located elsewhere.

4. Transit of a missile or launcher subject to the provisions of this Treaty shall be completed within 25 days.

5. All deployment areas, missile operating bases and missile support facilities are specified in the Memorandum of Understanding or in subsequent updates of data pursuant to paragraphs 3, 5(a) or 5(b) of Article IX of this Treaty. Neither Party shall increase the number of, or change the location or boundaries of, deployment areas, missile operating bases or missile support facilities, except for elimination facilities, from those set forth in the Memorandum of Understanding. A missile support facility shall not be considered to be part of a deployment area even though it may be located within the geographic boundaries of a deployment area.

6. Beginning 30 days after entry into force of this Treaty, neither Party shall locate intermediate-range or shorter-range missiles, including stages of such missiles, or launchers of such missiles at missile production facilities, launcher production facilities or test ranges listed in the Memorandum of Understanding.

7. Neither Party shall locate any intermediate-range or shorter-range missiles at training facilities.

8. A non-deployed intermediate-range or shorter-range missile shall not be carried on or contained within a launcher of such a type of missile, except as required for maintenance conducted at repair facilities or for elimination by means of launching conducted at elimination facilities.

9. Training missiles and training launchers for intermediate-range or shorter-range missiles shall be subject to the same locational restrictions as are set forth for intermediate-range and shorter-range missiles and launchers of such missiles in paragraphs 1 and 3 of this Article.

Article IX

1. The Memorandum of Understanding contains categories of data relevant to obligations undertaken with regard to this Treaty and lists all intermediate-range and shorter-range missiles, launchers of such missiles, and support structures and support equipment associated with such missiles and launchers, possessed by the Parties as of November 1, 1987. Updates of that data and notifications required by this Article shall be provided according to the categories of data contained in the Memorandum of Understanding.

2. The Parties shall update that data and provide the notifications required by this Treaty through the Nuclear Risk Reduction Centers, established pursuant to the Agreement Between the United States of America and the Union of Soviet Socialist Republics on the Establishment of Nuclear Risk Reduction Centers of September 15, 1987.

3. No later than 30 days after entry into force of this Treaty, each Party shall provide the other Party with updated data, as of the date of entry

into force of this Treaty, for all categories of data contained in the Memorandum of Understanding.

4. No later than 30 days after the end of each six-month interval following the entry into force of this Treaty, each Party shall provide updated data for all categories of data contained in the Memorandum of Understanding by informing the other Party of all changes, completed and in process, in that data, which have occurred during the six-month interval since the preceding data exchange, and the net effect of those changes.

5. Upon entry into force of this Treaty and thereafter, each Party shall provide the following notifications to the other Party:

(a) notification, no less than 30 days in advance, of the scheduled date of the elimination of a specific deployment area, missile operating base or missile support facility;

(b) notification, no less than 30 days in advance, of changes in the number or location of elimination facilities, including the location and scheduled date of each change;

(c) notification, except with respect to launches of intermediate-range missiles for the purpose of their elimination, no less than 30 days in advance, of the scheduled date of the initiation of the elimination of intermediate-range and shorter-range missiles, and stages of such missiles, and launchers of such missiles and support structures and support equipment associated with such missiles and launchers, including:

(i) the number and type of items of missile systems to be eliminated;

(ii) the elimination site;

(iii) for intermediate-range missiles, the location from which such missiles, launchers of such missiles and support equipment associated with such missiles and launchers are moved to the elimination facility; and

(iv) except in the case of support structures, the point of entry to be used by an inspection team conducting an inspection pursuant to paragraph 7 of Article XI of this Treaty and the estimated time of departure of an inspection team from the point of entry to the elimination facility;

(d) notification, no less than ten days in advance, of the scheduled date of the launch, or the scheduled date of the initiation of a series of launches, of intermediate-range missiles for the purpose of their elimination, including:

(i) the type of missiles to be eliminated;

(ii) the location of the launch, or, if elimination is by a series of launches, the location of such launches and the number of launches in the series;

(iii) the point of entry to be used by an inspection team conducting an inspection pursuant to paragraph 7 of Article XI of this Treaty; and

(iv) the estimated time of departure of an inspection team from the point of entry to the elimination facility;

(e) notification, no later than 48 hours after they occur, of changes in the number of intermediate-range and shorter-range missiles, launchers of such missiles and support structures and support equipment associated with such missiles and launchers resulting from elimination as described in the Protocol on Elimination, including:

(i) the number and type of items of a missile system which were eliminated; and

(ii) the date and location of such elimination; and

(f) notification of transit of intermediate-range or shorter-range missiles or launchers of such missiles, or the movement of training missiles or training launchers for such intermediate-range and shorter-range missiles, no later than 48 hours after it has been completed, including:

(i) the number of missiles or launchers;

(ii) the points, dates, and times of departure and arrival;

(iii) the mode of transport; and

(iv) the location and time at that location at least once every four days during the period of transit.

6. Upon entry into force of this Treaty and thereafter, each Party shall notify the other Party, no less than ten days in advance, of the scheduled

date and location of the launch of a research and development booster system as described in paragraph 12 of Article VII of this Treaty.

Article X

1. Each Party shall eliminate its intermediate-range and shorter-range missiles and launchers of such missiles and support structures and support equipment associated with such missiles and launchers in accordance with the procedures set forth in the Protocol on Elimination.

2. Verification by on-site inspection of the elimination of items of missile systems specified in the Protocol on Elimination shall be carried out in accordance with Article XI of this Treaty, the Protocol on Elimination and the Protocol on Inspection.

3. When a Party removes its intermediate-range missiles, launchers of such missiles and support equipment associated with such missiles and launchers from deployment areas to elimination facilities for the purpose of their elimination, it shall do so in complete deployed organizational units. For the United States of America, these units shall be Pershing II batteries and BGM-109G flights. For the Union of Soviet Socialist Republics, these units shall be SS-20 regiments composed of two or three battalions.

4. Elimination of intermediate-range and shorter-range missiles and launchers of such missiles and support equipment associated with such missiles and launchers shall be carried out at the facilities that are specified in the Memorandum of Understanding or notified in accordance with paragraph 5(b) of Article IX of this Treaty, unless eliminated in accordance with Sections IV or V of the Protocol on Elimination. Support structures, associated with the missiles and launchers subject to this Treaty, that are subject to elimination shall be eliminated in situ.

5. Each Party shall have the right, during the first six months after entry into force of this Treaty, to eliminate by means of launching no more than 100 of its intermediate-range missiles.

6. Intermediate-range and shorter-range missiles which have been tested prior to entry into force of this Treaty, but never deployed, and

which are not existing types of intermediate-range or shorter-range missiles listed in Article III of this Treaty, and launchers of such missiles, shall be eliminated within six months after entry into force of this Treaty in accordance with the procedures set forth in the Protocol on Elimination. Such missiles are:

(a) for the United States of America, missiles of the type designated by the United States of America as the Pershing IB, which is known to the Union of Soviet Socialist Republics by the same designation; and

(b) for the Union of Soviet Socialist Republics, missiles of the type designated by the Union of Soviet Socialist Republics as the RK-55, which is known to the United States of America as the SSC-X-4.

7. Intermediate-range and shorter-range missiles and launchers of such missiles and support structures and support equipment associated with such missiles and launchers shall be considered to be eliminated after completion of the procedures set forth in the Protocol on Elimination and upon the notification provided for in paragraph 5(e) of Article IX of this Treaty.

8. Each Party shall eliminate its deployment areas, missile operating bases and missile support facilities. A Party shall notify the other Party pursuant to paragraph 5(a) of Article IX of this Treaty once the conditions set forth below are fulfilled:

(a) all intermediate-range and shorter-range missiles, launchers of such missiles and support equipment associated with such missiles and launchers located there have been removed;

(b) all support structures associated with such missiles and launchers located there have been eliminated; and

(c) all activity related to production, flight-testing, training, repair, storage or deployment of such missiles and launchers has ceased there.

Such deployment areas, missile operating bases and missile support facilities shall be considered to be eliminated either when they have been inspected pursuant to paragraph 4 of Article XI of this Treaty or when 60 days have elapsed since the date of the scheduled elimination which was notified pursuant to paragraph 5(a) of Article IX of this Treaty. A deployment area, missile operating base or missile support facility listed in the Memorandum of Understanding that met the above conditions prior to entry into force of this Treaty, and is not included in the initial data exchange pursuant to paragraph 3 of Article IX of this Treaty, shall be considered to be eliminated.

9. If a Party intends to convert a missile operating base listed in the Memorandum of Understanding for use as a base associated with GLBM or GLCM systems not subject to this Treaty, then that Party shall notify the other Party, no less than 30 days in advance of the scheduled date of the initiation of the conversion, of the scheduled date and the purpose for which the base will be converted.

Article XI

1. For the purpose of ensuring verification of compliance with the provisions of this Treaty, each Party shall have the right to conduct on-site inspections. The Parties shall implement on-site inspections in accordance with this Article, the Protocol on Inspection and the Protocol on Elimination.

2. Each Party shall have the right to conduct inspections provided for by this Article both within the territory of the other Party and within the territories of basing countries.

3. Beginning 30 days after entry into force of this Treaty, each Party shall have the right to conduct inspections at all missile operating bases and missile support facilities specified in the Memorandum of Understanding other than missile production facilities, and at all elimination facilities included in the initial data update required by paragraph 3 of Article IX of this Treaty. These inspections shall be completed no later than 90 days after entry into force of this Treaty. The purpose of these inspections shall be to verify the number of missiles, launchers, support structures and support equipment and other data, as of the date of entry into force of this Treaty, provided pursuant to paragraph 3 of Article IX of this Treaty.

4. Each Party shall have the right to conduct inspections to verify the elimination, notified pursuant to paragraph 5(a) of Article IX of this Treaty, of missile operating bases and missile support facilities other than missile production facilities, which are thus no longer subject to inspections pursuant to paragraph 5(a) of this Article. Such an inspection shall be carried out within 60 days after the scheduled date of the elimination of that facility. If a Party conducts an inspection at a particular facility pursuant to paragraph 3 of this Article after the scheduled date of the elimination of that facility, then no additional inspection of that facility pursuant to this paragraph shall be permitted.

5. Each Party shall have the right to conduct inspections pursuant to this paragraph for 13 years after entry into force of this Treaty. Each Party shall have the right to conduct 20 such inspections per calendar year during the first three years after entry into force of this Treaty, 15 such inspections per calendar year during the subsequent five years, and ten such inspections per calendar year during the last five years. Neither Party shall use more than half of its total number of these inspections per calendar year within the territory of any one basing country. Each Party shall have the right to conduct:

(a) inspections, beginning 90 days after entry into force of this Treaty, of missile operating bases and missile support facilities other than elimination facilities and missile production facilities, to ascertain, according to the categories of data specified in the Memorandum of Understanding, the numbers of missiles, launchers, support structures and support equipment located at each missile operating base or missile support facility at the time of the inspection; and

(b) inspections of former missile operating bases and former missile support facilities eliminated pursuant to paragraph 8 of Article X of this Treaty other than former missile production facilities.

6. Beginning 30 days after entry into force of this Treaty, each Party shall have the right, for 13 years after entry into force of this Treaty, to inspect by means of continuous monitoring:

(a) the portals of any facility of the other Party at which the final assembly of a GLBM using stages, any of which is outwardly similar to a stage of a solid-propellant GLBM listed in Article III of this Treaty, is accomplished; or

(b) if a Party has no such facility, the portals of an agreed former missile production facility at which existing types of intermediate-range or shorter-range GLBMs were produced.

The Party whose facility is to be inspected pursuant to this paragraph shall ensure that the other Party is able to establish a permanent continuous monitoring system at that facility within six months after entry into force of this Treaty or within six months of initiation of the process of final assembly described in subparagraph (a). If, after the end of the second year after entry into force of this Treaty, neither Party conducts the process of final assembly described in subparagraph (a) for a period of 12 consecutive months, then neither Party shall have the right to inspect by means of continuous monitoring any missile production facility of the other Party unless the process of final assembly as described in subparagraph (a) is initiated again. Upon entry into force of this Treaty, the facilities to be inspected by continuous monitoring shall be: in accordance with subparagraph (b), for the United States of America, Hercules Plant Number 1, at Magna, Utah; in accordance with subparagraph (a), for the Union of Soviet Socialist Republics, the Votkinsk Machine Building Plant, Udmurt Autonomous Soviet Socialist Republic, Russian Soviet Federative Socialist Republic.

7. Each Party shall conduct inspections of the process of elimination, including elimination of intermediate-range missiles by means of launching, of intermediate-range and shorter-range missiles and launchers of such missiles and support equipment associated with such missiles and launchers carried out at elimination facilities in accordance with Article X of this Treaty and the Protocol on Elimination. Inspectors conducting inspections provided for in this paragraph shall determine that the processes specified for the elimination of the missiles, launchers and support equipment have been completed.

8. Each Party shall have the right to conduct inspections to confirm the completion of the process of elimination of intermediate-range and shorter-range missiles and launchers of such missiles and support

equipment associated with such missiles and launchers eliminated pursuant to Section V of the Protocol on Elimination, and of training missiles, training missile stages, training launch canisters and training launchers eliminated pursuant to Sections II, IV and V of the Protocol on Elimination.

Article XII

1. For the purpose of ensuring verification of compliance with the provisions of this Treaty, each Party shall use national technical means of verification at its disposal in a manner consistent with generally recognized principles of international law.

2. Neither Party shall:

(a) interfere with national technical means of verification of the other Party operating in accordance with paragraph 1 of this Article; or

(b) use concealment measures which impede verification of compliance with the provisions of this Treaty by national technical means of verification carried out in accordance with paragraph 1 of this Article. This obligation does not apply to cover or concealment practices, within a deployment area, associated with normal training, maintenance and operations, including the use of environmental shelters to protect missiles and launchers.

3. To enhance observation by national technical means of verification, each Party shall have the right until a Treaty between the Parties reducing and limiting strategic offensive arms enters into force, but in any event for no more than three years after entry into force of this Treaty, to request the implementation of cooperative measures at deployment bases for road-mobile GLBMs with a range capability in excess of 5500 kilometers, which are not former missile operating bases eliminated pursuant to paragraph 8 of Article X of this Treaty. The Party making such a request shall inform the other Party of the deployment base at which cooperative measures shall be implemented. The Party whose base is to be observed shall carry out the following cooperative measures:

(a) no later than six hours after such a request, the Party shall have opened the roofs of all fixed structures for launchers located at the base, removed completely all missiles on launchers from such fixed structures for launchers and displayed such missiles on launchers in the open without using concealment measures; and

(b) the Party shall leave the roofs open and the missiles on launchers in place until twelve hours have elapsed from the time of the receipt of a request for such an observation.

Each Party shall have the right to make six such requests per calendar year. Only one deployment base shall be subject to these cooperative measures at any one time.

Article XIII

1. To promote the objectives and implementation of the provisions of this Treaty, the Parties hereby establish the Special Verification Commission. The Parties agree that, if either Party so requests, they shall meet within the framework of the Special Verification Commission to:

(a) resolve questions relating to compliance with the obligations assumed; and

(b) agree upon such measures as may be necessary to improve the viability and effectiveness of this Treaty.

2. The Parties shall use the Nuclear Risk Reduction Centers, which provide for continuous communication between the Parties, to:

(a) exchange data and provide notifications as required by paragraphs 3, 4, 5 and 6 of Article IX of this Treaty and the Protocol on Elimination;

(b) provide and receive the information required by paragraph 9 of Article X of this Treaty;

(c) provide and receive notifications of inspections as required by Article XI of this Treaty and the Protocol on Inspection; and

(d) provide and receive requests for cooperative measures as provided for in paragraph 3 of Article XII of this Treaty.

Article XIV

The Parties shall comply with this Treaty and shall not assume any international obligations or undertakings which would conflict with its provisions.

Article XV

1. This Treaty shall be of unlimited duration.

2. Each Party shall, in exercising its national sovereignty, have the right to withdraw from this Treaty if it decides that extraordinary events related to the subject matter of this Treaty have jeopardized its supreme interests. It shall give notice of its decision to withdraw to the other Party six months prior to withdrawal from this Treaty. Such notice shall include a statement of the extraordinary events the notifying Party regards as having jeopardized its supreme interests.

Article XVI

Each Party may propose amendments to this Treaty. Agreed amendments shall enter into force in accordance with the procedures set forth in Article XVII governing the entry into force of this Treaty.

Article XVII

1. This Treaty, including the Memorandum of Understanding and Protocols, which form an integral part thereof, shall be subject to ratification in accordance with the constitutional procedures of each Party. This Treaty shall enter into force on the date of the exchange of instruments of ratification.

2. This Treaty shall be registered pursuant to Article 102 of the Charter of the United Nations.

DONE at Washington on December 8, 1987, in two copies, each in the English and Russian languages, both texts being equally authentic.

FOR THE UNITED STATES OF AMERICA:

Ronald Reagan

President of the United States of America

FOR THE UNION OF SOVIET SOCIALIST REPUBLICS:

Mikhail Gorbachev

General Secretary of the Central Committee of the CPSU

The Joint Russian-United States Statement on the INF Treaty[1]

STATEMENT by Vitaly I. Churkin, the Russian Federation's Permanent Representative to the UN, in the UN General Assembly's First Committee Introducing the Joint Russian-United States Statement on the INF Treaty

October 25, 2007

Mr. Chairman,

Today in the First Committee of the UN General Assembly the delegations of the Russian Federation and the United States of America circulated the text of the Joint Russian-US Statement on the Treaty on the Elimination of Intermediate-Range and Shorter-Range Missiles. In this connection the Russian delegation would like to make the following statement.

The publication by Russia and the United States of the Joint Statement on this question coincides with the approaching twentieth anniversary of the signing of the Treaty between the USSR and the USA on the Elimination of Their Intermediate-Range (from 1,000 to

---

[1] Ministry of Foreign Affairs of the Russian Federation, Information and Press Department, "STATEMENT by Vitaly I. Churkin, the Russian Federation's Permanent Representative to the UN, in the UN General Assembly's First Committee Introducing the Joint Russian-United States Statement on the INF Treaty," Moscow, Russia, October 25, 2007. Online at http://www.un.int/russia/new/MainRoot/docs/off_news/291007/newen1.htm, as of April 2012.

5,500 km) and Shorter-Range (500 to 1,000 km) Missiles. It is impossible to overestimate the historic significance of this international legal act: it marked an important, practical step for them towards meeting their article VI obligation under the Treaty on the Nonproliferation of Nuclear Weapons to pursue negotiations on nuclear-missile disarmament.

By June 1, 1991, under the Treaty, the USSR destroyed 1846 intermediate and shorter-range missiles and 825 launchers for them along with relevant infrastructure and auxiliary equipment. The US, by the same deadline, destroyed 846 intermediate and shorter-range missiles, 289 launchers for them and all supporting infrastructure.

The Treaty on the Elimination of Intermediate-Range and Shorter-Range Missiles opened the way for the subsequent conclusion of the Treaty on the Reduction and Limitation of Strategic Offensive Arms, thus lowering the dangerously high level of confrontation between the two leading nuclear powers and ensured movement forward along the road of strengthening mutual trust and overcoming the relicts of the Cold War. The conclusion of the Treaty on the Elimination of Intermediate-Range and Shorter-Range Missiles helped to substantially decrease international tensions, particularly in Europe.

As the Joint Statement stresses, Russia and the United States are convinced that, in today's conditions, the Treaty retains its long-standing importance and reaffirm their joint support for this document.

Addressed to all states participants of the 62nd UNGA Session, the Joint Statement reflects our countries' concern over the situation in the field of the proliferation of intermediate and shorter-range missiles, since an ever greater number of countries are acquiring or trying to acquire missile production technologies and adding such missiles to their arsenals. A paradoxical situation evolves where the Treaty on the Elimination of Intermediate-Range and Shorter-Range Missiles, of unlimited duration, is limiting the actions of only a few states, primarily Russia and the United States.

To reverse these alarming tendencies, objectively leading to increased international tensions, the Russian Federation and the US call on all interested countries to discuss the possibility of imparting a global character to the obligations under the Treaty on the Elimination of Intermediate-Range and Shorter-Range Missiles. That understanding would take into account the contemporary realities and help to strengthen the nuclear-missile nonproliferation regime.

We think that renunciation of intermediate and shorter-range missiles, leading to the elimination of this class of missiles and cessation of associated programs, could help the enhancement of the Treaty's role as a factor for bolstering international security and strategic stability.

Mr. Chairman,

In conclusion I would like to draw attention to the fact that the Russian Federation and the United States in the document circulated today have declared their resolve to work with all interested countries and make every effort to prevent the proliferation of intermediate and shorter-range missiles and strengthen peace in the world. We count on a constructive response from member states to our joint initiative.

Thank you for your attention.

Bibliography

Arbatov, Alexei. *Gambit or Endgame? The New State of Arms Control*. Washington: Carnegie Endowment for International Peace, 2011.

————. "Missile Defense and the Intermediate Nuclear Forces Treaty." International Commission on Nuclear Non-proliferation and Disarmament, 2009.

"Arsenal Ship." Federation of American Scientists. No Date. As of August 21, 2012: http://www.fas.org/programs/ssp/man/uswpns/navy/surfacewarfare/arsenalship.html

Baker, Peter. "Senate Passes Arms Control Treaty with Russia, 71-26." *New York Times*, December 22, 2010.

Blair, Dennis C. "Annual Threat Assessment of the US Intelligence Community for the Senate Select Committee on Intelligence," Director of National Intelligence, February 2, 2010.

Boese, Wade. "Interdiction Initiative Successes Assessed." *Arms Control Today*, June/August 2008.

Bolton, John R., and Paula A. DeSutter. "A Cold War Missile Treaty That's Doing Us Harm: The U.S.-Soviet INF Pact Doesn't Address the Iranian Threat." *Wall Street Journal*, August 15, 2011, p. 11.

Borger, Julian. "Five NATO States to Urge Removal of US Nuclear Arms in Europe." *Guardian*, Feburary 23, 2010, p. 19.

Boudreaux, Richard. "Russia's Fading Army Fights Losing Battle to Reform Itself." *Wall Street Journal*, April 20, 2011.

Bowen, Wyn. "U.S. Policy on Ballistic Missile Proliferation: The MTCR's First Decade (1987-1997)." *Nonproliferation Review,* 1997, pp. 21-39.

Brookes, Peter. "New START Treaty's China Challenge." *New York Post*, September 20, 2010.

Cha, Victor D. "What Do They Really Want?: Obama's North Korea Conundrum." *Washington Quarterly*, Vol. 32, No. 4, 2009, pp. 119–138.

Champlin, Luke, and Volha Charnysh. "Russia Plans Changes to Military Doctrine." *Arms Control Today*, December 2009.

Charnysh, Volha. "Russian Nuclear Threshold Not Lowered." *Arms Control Today*, March 2010.

Chayes, Antonia. "How American Treaty Behavior Threatens National Security." *International Security*, Vol. 33, No. 1, 2008, pp. 45–81.

Chivvis, Christopher. *Recasting NATO's Strategic Concept: Possible Directions for the United States*. Santa Monica, Calif.: RAND Corporation, OP-280-AF, 2009. As of August 20, 2012:
http://www.rand.org/pubs/occasional_papers/OP280.html

Cliff, Roger, Mark Burles, Michael S. Chase, Derek Eaton, and Kevin L. Pollpeter. *Entering the Dragon's Lair: Chinese Antiaccess Strategies and Their Implications for the United States*. Santa Monica, Calif.: RAND Corporation, MG-524-AF, 2007. As of August 20, 2012:
http://www.rand.org/pubs/monographs/MG524.html

Cohen, Eliot A. "Toward Better Net Assessment: Rethinking the European Conventional Balance." *International Security*, Vol. 13, No. 1, 1988, pp. 50–89.

Collina, Tom Z. "Russia Below Some New START Limits." *Arms Control Today*, July/August 2011.

Davis, Lynn E. "Lessons of the INF Treaty." *Foreign Affairs*, Vol. 66, 1987-88, pp. 720–734.

Davis, Lynn E., Jeffrey Martini, Alireza Nader, Dalia Dassa Kaye, James T. Quinlivan, and Paul Steinberg. *Iran's Nuclear Future: Critical U.S. Policy Choices*. Santa Monica, Calif.: RAND Corporation, MG-1087-AF, 2011. As of August 20, 2012:
http://www.rand.org/pubs/monographs/MG1087.html

Diakov, Anatoli, and Frank von Hippel. *Challenges and Opportunities for Russia-U.S. Nuclear Arms Control*. Washington: The Century Foundation, 2009.

Dinmore, Guy, Demetri Sevastopulo, and Hubert Wetzel. "Russia Confronted Rumsfeld with Threat to Quit Treaty." *Financial Times*, March 9, 2005, p. 1.

Dvorkin, Vladamir. "Reducing Russia's Reliance on Nuclear Weapons in Security Policies." In *Engaging China and Russia on Nuclear Disarmament*, edited by Cristina Hansell and William C. Potter, Monterey: James Martin Center for Nonproliferation Studies, 2009, pp. 89–102.

Edelman, Eric, Andrew Krepinevich, and Evan Braden Montgomery. "The Dangers of a Nuclear Iran." *Foreign Affairs*, Vol. 90, No. 1, 2011.

Elleman, Michael. "Containing Iran's Missile Threat." *Survival,* Vol. 54, No. 1, 2012, pp. 119–126.

Erickson, Andrew S., and David D. Yang. "On the Verge of a Game-Changer." *Proceedings Magazine,* Vol. 135, No. 5, 2009.

———. "Using the Land to Control the Sea?: Chinese Analysts Consider the Antiship Ballistic Missile." *Naval War College Review,* Vol. 62, No. 4, 2009, pp. 53–86.

"Fact Sheet: The Missile Technology Control Regime at a Glance." Arms Control Association, August 2012. As of August 2012:
http://www.armscontrol.org/factsheets/mtcr

"Fact Sheet: Worlwide Ballistic Missile Inventories." Arms Control Association, January 2012. As of August 2012:
http://www.armscontrol.org/factsheets/missiles

Fedyszyn, Thomas. "Saving NATO: Renunciation of the Article 5 Guarantee." *Orbis,* Vol. 54, No. 3, 2010, pp. 374–386.

Feickert, Andrew. "Missile Technology Control Regime (MTCR) and International Code of Conduct against Ballistic Missile Proliferation (ICOC): Background and Issues for Congress." Washington: Congressional Research Service, April 8, 2003.

"Final Report." *The Commission to Assess the Ballistic Missile Threat to the United States,* July 15, 1998.

Fitzpatrick, Mark. "North Korean Security Challenges: A Net Assessment." Washington: International Institute for Strategic Studies, 2011.

———, ed. *Iran's Ballistic Missile Capabilities: A Net Assessment.* London: International Institute for Strategic Studies, 2010.

Flynn, Kevin. "Medvedev Delivers Chilling Words on Missile Plans." *Independent,* November 5, 2008.

Fravel, M. Taylor, and Evan S. Medeiros. "China's Search for Assured Retaliation: The Evolution of Chinese Nuclear Strategy and Force Structure." *International Security,* Vol. 35, No. 2, 2010, pp. 48–87.

George, Alexander, and Richard Smoke. *Deterrence in American Foreign Policy: Theory and Practice.* New York: Columbia University Press, 1974.

Gertler, Jeremiah J. *Air Force Next-Generation Bomber: Background and Issues for Congress.* Washington: Congressional Research Service, 2009.

Glitman, Maynard W. *The Last Battle of the Cold War: An Inside Account of Negotiating the Intermediate Range Nuclear Forces Treaty.* New York: Palgrave Macmillan, 2006.

Goldgeier, James M. *The Future of NATO*. New York: Council on Foreign Relations, 2010.

———. "NATO's Future: Facing Old Divisions and New Threats." *Harvard International Review*, July 2009.

Gormley, Dennis M., *Missile Contagion: Cruise Missile Proliferation and the Threat to International Security*. Annapolis: Naval Institute Press, 2008.

———. "Winning on Ballistic Missiles but Losing on Cruise: The Missile Proliferation Battle." *Arms Control Today*, December 2009.

Gries, Peter Hays. "Problems of Misperception in U.S.-China Relations." *Orbis*, Vol. 53, No. 2, 2009, pp. 220–232.

Gunzinger, Mark. *Sustaining America's Advantage in Long-Range Strike*. Washington: Center for Strategic and Budgetary Assessments, 2010.

Haffa, Robert, and Michael Isherwood. *The 2018 Bomber: The Case for Accelerating the Next Generation Long-Range Strike System*. Washington: Northrop Grumman, 2008.

Halpin, Tony. "Putin Confronts US with Threat to Arms Pact." *Times (London)*, October 13, 2007, p. 54.

Hansell, Cristina, and Nikita Perfilyev. "Strategic Relations between the United States, Russia, and China and the Possibility of Cooperation on Disarmament." In *Engaging China and Russia on Nuclear Disarmament*, edited by Cristina Hansell and William C. Potter, Monterey: James Martin Center for Nonproliferation Studies, 2009, pp. 123–148.

Harding, Luke. "Kremlin Tears up Arms Pact with NATO: Russia's Relations with West Hit a New Low Point." *The Observer (On-line)*, July 14, 2007. As of August 20, 2012:
http://www.guardian.co.uk/world/2007/jul/15/russia.nato/print

———. "Putin Threatens Withdrawal from Cold War Treaty." *Guardian*, October 12, 2007.

Harvey, John R. "Ballistic Missiles and Advanced Strike Aircraft: Comparing Military Effectiveness." *International Security*, Vol. 17, No. 2, 1992, pp. 41–83.

Hildreth, Steven A. "Iran's Ballistic Missile Programs: An Overview." Washington: Congressional Research Service, 2009.

———. "North Korean Ballistic Missile Threat to the United States." Washington: Congressional Research Service, 2009.

Hildreth, Steven A., and Carl Eck. "Long-Range Ballistic Missile Defense in Europe." Washington: Congressional Research Service, 2009.

Hoehn, Andrew R., and Sarah Harting. *Risking NATO: Testing the Limits of the Alliance in Afghanistan.* Santa Monica, Calif.: RAND Corporation, MG-974-AF, 2010. As of August 20, 2012:
http://www.rand.org/pubs/monographs/MG974.html

Holloway, David. *The Soviet Union and the Arms Race.* New Haven: Yale University Press, 1984.

Hoyler, Marshall. "China's 'Antiaccess' Ballistic Missiles and U.S. Active Defenses." *Naval War College Review,* Vol. 63, No. 4, 2010, pp. 84–105.

Hughes, Christopher W. *Japan's Remilitarization.* London: International Institute for Strategic Studies, 2009.

Huth, Paul K. *Extended Deterrence and the Prevention of War.* New Haven: Yale University Press, 1988.

"INF Treaty Pullout May Lead to New Arms Race—Russian General." *BBC Worldwide Monitoring,* February 19, 2007.

"Iran's Nucelar and Missile Potential: A Joint Threat Assessment by U.S. and Russian Technical Experts." New York: East West Institute, 2009.

"Is Russia Bluffing on Nuclear Treaty?" *Jane's Intelligence Digest,* October 29, 2007.

Isby, David C. "Extended-Range Iskander Could Break INF Treaty." *Jane's Missiles & Rockets,* January 1, 2008.

Johnson, Stuart E., and Duncan Long, eds. *Coping with the Dragon: Essays of PLA Transformation and the U.S. Military.* Washington: National Defense University, 2007.

Kan, Shirley A. *China and Proliferation of Weapons of Mass Destruction and Missiles: Policy Issues.* Washington: Congressional Research Service, 2011.

Khorunzhiy, Nikolai. "Should Russia Quit Treaty on Medium- and Short-Range Missiles?" *RIA Novosti (On-Line),* November 4, 2007.

———. "Should Russia Quit the Treaty on Medium- and Short-Range Missiles?" *RIA Novosti,* April 11, 2007.

Kim, Sunhyuk, and Wonhyuk Lim. "How to Deal with South Korea." *Washington Quarterly,* Vol. 30, No. 2, 2007, pp. 71–82.

Kislyakov, Andrei. "A Bad Treaty Is Better Than a Good Missile." *McClatchy-Tribune News Service,* February 21, 2007.

Klinger, Bruce. "Backgrounder No. 2506: The Case for Comprehensive Missile Defense in Asia." Heritage Foundation, January 7, 2011.

Kramer, Andrew E., and Thom Shanker. "Russia Steps Back from Key Arms Treaty." *New York Times,* July 14, 2007.

Kramer, David J. "Resetting U.S.-Russian Relations: It Takes Two." *Washington Quarterly,* Vol. 33, No. 1, 2010, pp. 61–79.

Krastev, Ivan, Mark Leonard, Dimitar Bechev, Jana Kobzova, and Andrew Wilson. *The Spectre of a Multipolar Europe.* London: European Council on Foreign Relations, 2010.

Krepinevich, Andrew. *Why Airsea Battle?* Washington: Center for Strategic and Budgetary Assessments, 2010.

Krepinevich, Andrew, Barry Watts, and Robert Work. *Meeting the Anti-Access and Area Denial Challenge.* Washington: Center for Strategic and Budgetary Assessments, 2003.

Lamond, Claudine, and Paul Ingram, "Politics around US Tactical Nuclear Weapons in European Host States," *BASIC Getting to Zero* Papers, No. 11.

Landler, Mark. "U.S. To Resist NATO Push to Remove Tactical Arms." *International Herald Tribune,* April 23, 2010, p. 5.

Larrabee, F. Stephen. "Whither Missile Defense?" *International Spectator,* Vol. 43, No. 2, 2008, pp. 5–13.

Larrabee, F. Stephen, and Christopher Chivvis. "Biden's Task in Eastern Europe: Reassurance." *Christian Science Monitor,* October 20, 2009.

Larrabee, F. Stephen, and David E. Mosher. "Rebuilding Arms Control." *United Press International,* August 10, 2007.

Leonard, Robert S., Jeffrey Drezner, and Geoffrey Sommer. *The Arsenal Ship Acquisition Process Experience: Contrasting and Common Impressions from the Contractor Teams and Joint Program Office.* Santa Monica, Calif.: RAND Corporation, MR-1030-DARPA, 1999. As of August 20, 2012: http://www.rand.org/pubs/monograph_reports/MR1030.html

Lewis, Jeffrey. "Chinese Nuclear Posture and Force Modernization." In *Engaging China and Russia on Nuclear Disarmament,* edited by Cristina Hansell and William C. Potter, Monterey: James Martin Center for Nonproliferation Studies, 2009, pp. 37–46.

———. *The Minumum Means of Reprisal: China's Search for Security in the Nuclear Age.* Cambridge: The MIT Press, 2007.

Lindsay, James M., and Ray Takeyh. "After Iran Gets the Bomb: Containment and Its Complications." *Foreign Affairs,* Vol. 89, No. 2, 2010, pp. 33–49.

Long, Austin. *Deterrence -- From Cold War to Long War: Lessons from Six Decades of RAND Research.* Santa Monica, Calif.: RAND Corporation, MG-636-OSD/AF, 2008. As of August 20, 2012: http://www.rand.org/pubs/monographs/MG636.html

Ludwig, Walter C. "A Cold Start for Hot Wars? The Indian Army's New Limited War Doctrine." *International Security,* Vol. 32, No. 3, 2007–2008, pp. 158–190.

Majumdar, Dave. "U.S. Air Force May Buy 175 Bombers." *Defense News*, January 24, 2011.

Malone, David M., and Rohan Mukherjee. "India and China: Conflict and Cooperation." *Survival*, Vol. 52, No. 1, 2010, pp. 137–158.

Manchanda, Arnav. "When Truth Is Stranger Than Fiction: The Able Archer Incident." *Cold War History*, Vol. 9, No. 1, 2009, pp. 111–133.

McFeatters, Dale. "NATO Should Keep Nukes." *Korea Times*, April 26, 2010.

Mearsheimer, John J. "Assessing the Conventional Balance: The 3:1 Rule and Its Critics." *International Security*, Vol. 13, No. 4, 1989, pp. 54–89.

———. *Conventional Deterrence*. Ithaca: Cornell University Press, 1985.

Mearsheimer, John J., Barry R. Posen, and Eliot A. Cohen. "Reassessing Net Assessment." *International Security*, Vol. 13, No. 4, 1989, pp. 128–179.

Medeiros, Evan S. *Chasing the Dragon: Assessing China's Export Controls for WMD-Related Goods and Technologies*. Santa Monica, Calif.: RAND Corporation, MG-353, 2005. As of August 20, 2012:
http://www.rand.org/pubs/monographs/MG353.html

———. *China's International Behavior: Activism, Opportunism, and Diversification*. Santa Monica, Calif.: RAND Corporation, MG-850-AF, 2009. As of August 20, 2012:
http://www.rand.org/pubs/monographs/MG850.html

———. "Strategic Hedging and the Future of Asia-Pacific Stability." *Washington Quarterly*, Vol. 29, No. 1, 2005, pp. 145–1467.

Medeiros, Evan S., Keith Crane, Eric Heginbotham, Norman D. Levin, Julia F. Lowell, Angel Rabasa, and Somi Seong. *Pacific Currents: The Responses of U.S. Allies and Security Partners in East Asia to China's Rise*. Santa Monica, Calif.: RAND Corporation, MG-736-AF, 2008. As of August 20, 2012:
http://www.rand.org/pubs/monographs/MG736.html

Michishita, Narushige. "Playing the Same Game: North Korea's Coercive Attempt at U.S. Reconciliation." *Washington Quarterly*, Vol. 32, No. 4, 2009, pp. 139–152.

The Military Balance 2011. London: International Institute for Strategic Studies.

Ministry of Foreign Affairs of the Russian Federation, Information and Press Department, "STATEMENT by Vitaly I. Churkin, the Russian Federation's Permanent Representative to the UN, in the UN General Assembly's First Committee Introducing the Joint Russian-United States Statement on the INF Treaty," Moscow, Russia, October 25, 2007. As of April 2012:
http://www.un.int/russia/new/MainRoot/docs/off_news/291007/newen1.htm

Mistry, Dinshaw. *Containing Missile Proliferation: Strategic Technology, Security Regimes, and International Cooperation in Arms Control*. Seattle: University of Washington Press, 2003.

————. "Tempering Optimism About Nuclear Deterrence in South Asia." *Security Studies*, Vol. 18, 2009, pp. 148–182.

Morgan, Forrest, Karl P. Mueller, Evan S. Medeiros, Kevin L. Pollpeter, and Roger Cliff. *Dangerous Thresholds: Managing Escalation in the 21st Century.* Santa Monica, Calif.: RAND Corporation, MG-614-AF, 2008. As of August 20, 2012: http://www.rand.org/pubs/monographs/MG614.html

Mulvenon, James C., and David Finklestein, eds. *China's Revolution in Doctrinal Affairs: Emerging Trends in the Operational Art of the Chinese People's Liberation Army.* Washington: CNA Corporation, 2005.

Mulvenon, James C., Murray Scot Tanner, Michael S. Chase, David Frelinger, David C. Gompert, Martin C. Libicki, and Kevin L. Pollpeter. *Chinese Responses to U.S. Military Transformation and Implications for the Department of Defense.* Santa Monica, Calif.: RAND Corporation, MG-340-OSD, 2006. As of August 20, 2012: http://www.rand.org/pubs/monographs/MG340.html

National Intelligence Council, *Foreign Missile Developments and the Ballistic Missile Threat through 2015.* Washington, December 2001.

Nitkin, Mary Beth. "North Korea's Nuclear Weapons: Technical Issues." Washington: Congressional Research Service, 2011.

"No Need for Medium-Range Missiles in Russia's Western Regions—Defence Ministry." *BBC Worldwide Monitoring*, July 18, 2007.

Office of the Secretary of Defense, *Annual Report to Congress: Military Power of the People's Republic of China*, 2010.

O'Rourke, Ronald. "Navy Aegis Ballistic Missile Defense (BMD) Program: Background and Issues for Congress." Washington: Congressional Research Service, 2010.

————. *Navy Aegis Ballistic Missile Defense (BMD) Program: Background and Issues for Congress.* Washington: Congressional Research Service, 2010.

Ochmanek, David, and Lowell H. Schwartz. *The Challenge of Nuclear-Armed Regional Adversaries.* Santa Monica, Calif.: RAND Corporation, MG-671-AF, 2008. As of August 20, 2012: http://www.rand.org/pubs/monographs/MG671.html

"Ohio-Class SSGN-726 Tactical Trident." *GlobalSecurity.Org*, 2011. As of August 20, 2012: http://www.globalsecurity.org/military/systems/ship/ssgn-726.htm

Oliker, Olga, Keith Crane, Lowell H. Schwartz, and Catherine Yusupov. *Russian Foreign Policy: Sources and Implications.* Santa Monica, Calif.: RAND Corporation, MG-768-AF, 2009. As of August 20, 2012: http://www.rand.org/pubs/monographs/MG768.html

Ozga, Deborah A. "A Chronology of the Missile Technology Control Regime." *Nonproliferation Review,* Winter 1994.

Pempel, T. J. "Japan's Search for the 'Sweet Spot': International Cooperation and Regional Security in Northeast Asia." *Orbis,* Vol. 55, No. 2, 2011, pp. 255–273.

Peters, John E., James Dickens, Derek Eaton, C. Christine Fair, Nina Hachigan, Theodore W. Karasik, Rollie Lal, Rachel M. Swanger, Gregory F. Treverton, and Charles Wolf Jr. *War and Escalation in South Asia.* Santa Monica, Calif.: RAND Corporation, MG-367-1-AF, 2006. As of August 20, 2012: http://www.rand.org/pubs/monographs/MG367-1.html

Petrov, Vladimir. "Russia Releases Draft of Global INF Treaty." *Jane's Defence Weekly,* February 22, 2008.

———. "Russia, US Issue Call for Widening of INF Treaty." *Jane's Defence Weekly,* November 7, 2007.

Pillsbury, Michael. *China Debates the Future Security Environment.* Honolulu: University Press of the Pacific, 2004.

———, ed. *Chinese Views of Future Warfare.* Honolulu: University Press of the Pacific, 2002.

Pincus, Walter. "Panel Urges Keeping U.S. Nuclear Arms in Europe." *Washington Post,* January 9, 2009, p. A7.

Pollack, Joshua. "Missile Control: A Multi-Decade Experiment in Nonproliferation." *Bulletin of the Atomic Scientists,* August 1, 2011.

Pomper, Miles, William Potter, and Nikolai Sokov. "Reducing Tactical Nuclear Weapons in Europe." *Survival,* Vol. 52, No. 1, 2010, pp. 75–96.

Posen, Barry R. "Measuring the European Conventional Balance: Coping with Complexity in Threat Assessment." *International Security,* Vol. 9, No. 3, 1984, pp. 47–88.

Ross, Robert S. "The 1995-96 Taiwan Strait Confrontation: Coercion, Credibility, and the Use of Force." *International Security,* Vol. 25, No. 2, 2000, pp. 87–123.

———. "Navigating the Taiwan Strait: Deterrence, Escalation Dominance, and U.S.-China Relations." *International Security,* Vol. 27, No. 2, 2002, pp. 48–85.

Rueckert, George L. *Global Double Zero: The INF Treaty from Its Origins to Implementation.* Westport: Greenwood Press, 1993.

"Russia and Arms Control: Vlad and MAD." *The Economist,* June 7, 2007.

"Russia 'May Deploy Missiles in Belarus.'" *Turkish Daily News,* November 15, 2007.

"Russia Would Benefit from Leaving INF Treaty, Say Analysts." *BBC Worldwide Monitoring,* February 15, 2007.

"Russian Defence Ministry Marks INF Treaty Anniversary, Backs Globalization." *BBC Worldwide Monitoring*, June 4, 2008.

"Russian Pundit Suggests INF Treaty Change to Allow Non-Nuclear-Capable Missiles." *BBC Worldwide Monitoring*, March 2, 2007.

Ryan, Kevin. "Expand or Scrap Missile Ban: A Cold War Treaty Has Opened a Gap in U.S. and Russian Security." *Los Angeles Times*, October 16, 2007.

Saalman, Lora. *China & the U.S. Nuclear Posture Review*. Washington: Carnegie Endowment for International Peace, 2011.

———. "How Chinese Analysts View Arms Control, Disarmament, and Nuclear Deterrence after the Cold War." In *Engaging China and Russia on Nuclear Disarmament*, edited by Cristina Hansell and William C. Potter, Monterey: James Martin Center for Nonproliferation Studies, 2009, pp. 47–72.

Samuels, Richard J. "Japan's Goldilock's Strategy." *Washington Quarterly*, Vol. 29, No. 4, 2006, pp. 111–127.

Sanchez, Alex. "The South American Defense Council, UNASUR, the Latin American Military and the Region's Political Process." Council on Hemispheric Affairs, October 1, 2008.

Schwartz, Stephen I., ed. *Atomic Audit: The Costs and Consequences of U.S. Nuclear Weapons Since 1940*. Washington: Brookings Institution Press, 1998.

Sheridan, Mary Beth. "U.S. to Send Envoy to North Korea to Consider Food Aid." *Washington Post*, May 20, 2011.

Shlapak, David A., David T. Orletsky, Toy I. Reid, Murray Scot Tanner, and Barry Wilson. *A Question of Balance: Political Context and Military Aspects of the China-Taiwan Dispute*. Santa Monica, Calif.: RAND Corporation, MG-888-SRF, 2009. As of August 20, 2012:
http://www.rand.org/pubs/monographs/MG888.html

Shlapak, David A., David T. Orletsky, and Barry Wilson. *Dire Strait?: Military Aspects of the China-Taiwan Confrontation and Options for U.S. Policy*. Santa Monica, Calif.: RAND Corporation, MR-1217-SRF, 2000. As of August 20, 2012:
http://www.rand.org/pubs/monograph_reports/MR1217.html

Shleifer, Andrei, and Daniel Treisman. "Why Moscow Says No - a Question of Russian Interests, Not Psychology." *Foreign Affairs*, Vol. 90, No. 1, 2011, pp. 122–138.

Shulsky, Abram N. *Deterrence Theory and Chinese Behavior*. Santa Monica, Calif.: RAND Corporation, MR-1161-AF, 2000. As of August 20, 2012:
http://www.rand.org/pubs/monograph_reports/MR1161.html

Shuster, Simon. "Russia Wants a Finger on Europe's Nuclear Shield." *Time (Online)*, March 25, 2011.

Sidhu, Waheguru Pal Singh. "Looking Back: The Missile Technology Control Regime." *Arms Control Today,* April 2007.

Snyder, Glenn. *Deterrence and Defense: Toward a Theory of National Security.* Princeton: Princeton University Press, 1961.

So-hyun, Kim. "Calls Mounting for Return of U.S. Tactical Nukes." *Korea Herald,* March 1, 2011.

Sokov, Nikolai. "The Evolving Role of Nuclear Weapons in Russia's Security Policy." In *Engaging China and Russia on Nuclear Disarmament,* edited by Cristina Hansell and William C. Potter, Monterey: James Martin Center for Nonproliferation Studies, 2009, pp. 73–88.

———. "The New, 2010 Russian Military Doctrine: The Nuclear Angle." Center for Nonproliferation Studies, February 5, 2010. As of August 20, 2012: http://cns.miis.edu/stories/100205_russian_nuclear_doctrine.htm

———. "Military Exercises in Russia: Naval Deterrence Failures Compensated by Strategic Rocket Success." Monterey: James Martin Center for Nonproliferation Studies, February 24, 2004.

Speier, Richard. "Missile Nonproliferation and Missile Defense: Fitting Them Together." *Arms Control Today,* November 2007.

Stokes, Mark, and Dan Blumenthal. "Can a Treaty Contain China's Missiles?" *Washington Post,* January 2, 2011, p. A15.

———. "Why China's Missiles Matter to Us." *Atlanta-Journal Constitution,* January 5, 2011, p. 15A.

Sunohara, Tsuyoshi. "The Anatomy of Japan's Shifting Security Orientation." *Washington Quarterly,* Vol. 33, No. 4, 2010, pp. 39–57.

Szabo, Stephen F. "Can Berlin and Washington Agree on Russia?" *Washington Quarterly,* Vol. 32, No. 4, 2009, pp. 23–41.

Talbott, Strobe. *Deadly Gambit: The Reagan Administration and the Stalemate in Nuclear Arms Control.* New York: Alfred A. Knopf, 1984.

Thompson, Mark. "U.S. Missiles Deployed near China Send a Message." *Time,* July 8, 2010. As of August 20, 2012: http://www.time.com/time/nation/article/0,8599,2002378,00.html

Trenin, Dmitri. "Russia's Spheres of Interest, Not Influence." *Washington Quarterly,* Vol. 32, No. 4, 2009, pp. 3–22.

Truver, Scott C. "Floating Arsenal to Be 21st Century Battleship." *International Defense Review,* Vol. 29, No. 7, 1996, p. 44.

"TV Commentator Urges Russia's Withdrawal from INF Treaty." *BBC Worldwide Monitoring,* April 2, 2007.

U.S. Department of Defense. *Selected Acquistion Report (SAR)*. November 12, 2010.

U.S. Department of State. *Proliferation Security Initiative (PSI)*. No date. As of August 21, 2012:
http://www.state.gov/t/isn/c10390.htm

U.S. State Department, "Treaty Between The United States Of America And The Union Of Soviet Socialist Republics On The Elimination Of Their Intermediate-Range And Shorter-Range Missiles (INF Treaty)," Washington, D.C., December 8, 1987. As of May 15, 2012:
http://www.state.gov/t/avc/trty/102360.htm

Valencia, Mark J. "The Proliferation Security Initiative: A Glass Half-Full." *Arms Control Today*, June 2007.

Van Tol, Jan, Mark Gunzinger, Andrew Krepinevich, and Jim Thomas. *Airsea Battle: A Point of Departure Operational Concept*. Washington: Center for Strategic and Budgetary Assessments, 2010.

Vasconcelos, Alvaro de, and Marcin Zaborowski, eds. *European Perspectives on the New American Foreign Policy Agenda*. Paris: European Union Institute for Security Studies, 2009.

———, eds., *The Obama Moment: European and American Perspectives*, Paris: European Union Institute for Security Studies, 2009.

Vick, Alan, Richard Moore, Bruce Pirnie, and John Stillion. *Aerospace Operations Against Elusive Ground Targets*. Santa Monica, Calif.: RAND Corporation, MR-1398-AF, 2001. As of August 20, 2012:
http://www.rand.org/pubs/monograph_reports/MR1398.html

Weir, Fred. "Russia's Renewed Focus on Kuril Islands Draws Japanese Ire." *Christian Science Monitor*, February 11, 2011.

Wetting, Gerhard. "The Last Soviet Offensive in the Cold War: Emergence and Development of the Campaign against NATO Euromissiles, 1979-1983." *Cold War History*, Vol. 9, No. 1, 2009, pp. 79–110.

Wilkening, Dean A. "Does Missile Defense in Europe Threaten Russia?" *Survival*, Vol. 54, No. 1, 2012, pp. 31–52.

Wilkening, Dean, and Kenneth Watman. *Nuclear Deterrence in a Regional Context*. Santa Monica, Calif.: RAND Corporation, MR-500-A/AF, 1995. As of August 20, 2012:
http://www.rand.org/pubs/monograph_reports/MR500.html

Wood, John. *Russia, the Asymmetric Threat to the United States*. Santa Barbara: Praeger, 2009.